I268401

Filling the Holes in Our Souls

CARING GROUPS THAT BUILD LASTING RELATIONSHIPS

PAUL MEIER, M.D.
GENE A. GETZ, Ph.D.
RICHARD A. MEIER, D.Min.
ALLEN R. DORAN, M.D.

MOODY PRESS
CHICAGO

Contents

Foreword

*F*or more than sixteen years, I have been part of a church staff known for its commitment to reaching the lost—non-churched Harry and Mary, as we affectionately refer to them. As God has blessed our efforts over these years, we have seen many people cross the line of faith and begin a personal relationship with God through His Son Jesus Christ. Hence, we have become known as a church for nonchurched people, a label we appreciate, given our goal of reaching non-churched people for Christ.

At the same time, however, we have been equally committed to strengthening the faith of those who are already "in Christ." Since the beginning of Willow Creek Community Church, we have been devoted to raising up fully devoted followers of Jesus. Toward that end, we focus our attention in two primary directions.

First, the New Community, our mid-week service devoted to worship and teaching for the believer. And second, our small groups ministry, which emphasizes growth in Christ through the building of relationships. Real life change, we believe, happens best in the context of people rubbing shoulders with one another. The small group format is so critical to the life of the church that we have instituted small groups throughout: for children, junior high and high school students, singles and couples.

We believe so strongly in small groups that we chose early on in our development to depart from the traditional Sunday school to a small group format. This was a risk at first, because it meant change. Sixteen years later, we would say that it was a good gamble. If you were to visit Willow Creek and interview those who serve on our staff, you would find that small groups have played a significant and life-altering role among our leaders.

Personally, my life has been more deeply affected in small groups than from any other source, apart from my private time with the Lord. It has been in small groups that I have developed my closest friendships and witnessed life transformation. In fact, of all the ministries that I have been involved in, none has produced greater fulfillment than that of God's activity through small groups.

It would be my hope that every person would find his or her way into a small group where the real issues of life can be discussed, wrestled with, and applied in the context of both God's truth and God's people. Were that hope to become a reality, seekers would find the Savior and believers would be revitalized to live authentically in Christ.

The book you now hold in your hands is an insightful exploration of the function and the benefits of the small group, written by men well qualified by their abundant experience in this field. May this book inspire you and, through you, motivate others to step out of the norm and risk an involvement that has proved to be life- and church-changing for the people of Willow Creek.

DON COUSINS
Associate Pastor
Willow Creek Community Church

---◆---
Preface

*E*ach weekday the Moody Broadcasting Network airs a
call-in talk show called "The Minirth-Meier Clinic." The
program originates from the headquarters of one of America's largest Christian counseling organizations, the Minirth-
Meier Clinic in suburban Dallas, Texas. Each day people call
me (Richard) and the other counselors with questions and
problems, expressing their frustrations. After giving general
guidance and advice, we often encourage callers to make
sure they are connected to one of the most important resources God has given to His people, that is, the close asso-

ciation, fellowship, and growth offered in a group of believers who love each other in the Lord. That means not only being connected with a Bible-teaching, evangelical church but also part of a smaller group within the church, where openness can encourage growth in the things of the Lord.

The surprise to us has been the large number of people who respond that their church does not have any provision for such fellowship and growth in a small group setting. Many say they attend Sunday school, and Sunday school classes are vital to growth and do meet real needs. However, sometimes the format of a Sunday school class is a lecture time without much interaction or personal application of the Word to actual hurts and struggles. Pastors have also expressed frustration with not being able to find a format they are comfortable with that would meet the growth and intimacy needs of their people.

Is there any supplement to the Sunday school concept, especially for adults? How can a pastor feel secure with small Bible study groups that he does not teach in the church family? How can he be assured that they will not become divisive? Could small groups strengthen the local church and help believers grow?

We believe the answer is the growth group concept presented in this book. In no way do we want to diminish the importance of Sunday preaching services, Sunday school, or other important activities in the church, but in the evangelical body we are not fully ministering to hurting members, meeting them where they are with biblical solutions.

The Body of Christ needs to function; the many "one anothers" in the Scripture need to be exercised. But churches are often structured in such a way that the personal encouragement and growth, both spiritual and emotional, of individual members have been slighted. We barely got by with that in the eighties, and we don't dare risk trying to get by with it in the nineties. As we draw closer to the return of our Lord, we can expect this world to become more threatening and stressful. We cannot lull ourselves to sleep thinking that the economy of the eighties will continue to be the economy of the nineties, or that the relative freedom from persecution most Christians in the West have experienced will continue in the future. Hard times may be ahead, just around the corner.

Unfortunately, many of our churches are not prepared for that. They need to gear up for a caring ministry, much like that described in the early chapters of Acts, especially chapter 2, where the early church meets in small groups and not only grows in grace but also provides support to one another emotionally, financially, and in other ways.

This book combines the insights of two Christian psychiatrists, a pastor, and a former pastor/now pastoral counselor (myself), all of whom have been involved directly in church growth groups for many years. The ideas are more than theories; they are based on actual experiences and will encourage the Body of Christ and especially those in leadership positions who are looking for new answers to help their people grow and to find support. This book is not the final work on growth groups in the church; it is a contribution to explain and to stimulate growth groups as a tool in the Body of Christ.

A word of caution. We are not advocating the small group approach as just another "program" to be added to an already overcrowded schedule. Rather, in established churches these concepts should be carefully integrated into the existent structures. It is our intent to provide some suggestions on how this might be done.

On the other hand, for those who are starting new churches, we would encourage you to look at the small group concept as an integral part of the overall structure of your new church. Many churches have substituted small groups for adult Sunday school classes. Other churches have developed combinations that do not add to the "all too often" syndrome of adding more meetings to the weekly schedule.

A final note. In this book the authors use the term *elder* to refer to lay pastors. However, in some churches, deacons actually function as small group leaders. (For a more thorough description of the authors' views of leadership, see *Sharpening the Focus of the Church*, by Gene Getz [Wheaton, Ill.: Victor, 1989], pp. 121-84.)

As I (Paul) look forward to the third millennium, trying to prepare for the new challenges ahead, I see an ever-increasing need for people to be loved—for Christians to reach out to their world in love.

We see six billion people here on planet Earth, who all have, to some extent, holes in their souls. And looking back, we can see that for many years our churches have been strong on doctrine, which is essential, and strong on evangelism, which is also essential, but weak on obeying and implementing the "one another" concepts that are also essential for Christian growth and development.

Three legs are important in a healthy local church: good Bible *doctrine* based on the inerrancy of Scripture, *evangelism* that brings lost people to Christ, and *fellowship* where the "one another" principles of the New Testament are practiced—loving one another, exhorting one another, confessing faults to one another, comforting one another, and rebuking one another. Every local church needs this third leg because that's where growth really takes place and where scriptural truth can really be applied. This has been the key to the growth of today's mega-churches.

Today we owe a great debt of gratitude to Gene Getz and Ray Stedman for reviving the small group movement back in the sixties. That's where I learned how defensive I was and how to be vulnerable and grow. I owe my current ministry to the small group movement and to those pioneers.

I hope this book will be a giant leap forward in that small group movement and that this growth will continue into the third millennium so that churches can strengthen the fellowship leg of their ministry while remaining faithful to evangelism and doctrine. It is my prayer that this will help Christians everywhere to become functional and efficient for Christ.

RICHARD MEIER, D.MIN.
PAUL MEIER, M.D.

Acknowledgments

*T*hank you to Iva and Lou Morelli, Nancy and Graham Lyons, Jerome Brock, Dave Shaw and Jack Warren, Jim and Becki Terral, Hazel and Charlie Merz, and Nancy and Dave Higgins, who were so gracious in sharing their small group experiences with us.

Paul Meier wishes to thank the other members of his growth group for their prayer support during this project: Judy and Dick Knox, Mary Anne and Joe Merwin, and Ev and John Schroeder.

We would like to thank Donna Fletcher Crow for her untold help and direction.

A word of special appreciation to our editor, R. Duncan Jaenicke of Moody Press, who had the original vision for this book, who brought us together with inspiring enthusiasm, and who is truly dedicated to the growth group revolution.

CHAPTER ONE

So What's a Small Group?

*Y*ou know what's a bummer, Mom?" Sixteen-year-old Jared slammed the door behind him as the family came home from church. "I looked around our class this morning, and I realized I don't have one single friend at church."

Susan Flavell dropped her Bible and books on the nearest table and tied an apron over her cream-colored dress. "What do you mean, you don't have any friends? There must be at least twenty kids in your youth group—probably closer to thirty."

Jared leaned on the counter, watching his mother pre-pare Sunday dinner. "Yeah, at least that many, and I know them all by name. And I say, 'Hi, John,' and John smiles and says, 'Hi, Jared,' and Karen waves and says, 'How's school?' and I say, 'Fine,' and Pastor Dan says, 'Does anyone have a prayer request this week?' Every Sunday it's the same. Acquaintances aren't friends."

Susan nodded somewhat distractedly as she took a chicken casserole out of the oven and smiled at her husband, David, who came in just then to put the ice water on the table. "Debbie," Susan called, "come set the table. Dinner's almost ready."

A few minutes later the family sat around the Sunday dinner table as David asked the blessing. Susan and David Flavell often laughed at what a traditional, even old-fashioned family they were—still having Sunday dinner the way they did when they were kids. But it was a tradition they enjoyed, especially because it brought the family together for a quiet time in their busy lives—a time when they could really talk.

Susan ladled a scoop of peas onto her plate, then handed them to her son. "Now, Jared, what's this about feeling friendless at church? You're such an outgoing person, I can't imagine your having a problem like that."

Jared repeated what he'd said earlier, and his dad listened with a frown, chewing slowly on his buttered whole wheat roll. "I don't get it. You went to that concert with the kids two weeks ago, and this morning they announced a pizza party—"

"*I've* got friends—Abby and Joye and Katie and—"

"Debbie, don't talk with your mouth full." Susan put her fork down. "David, I think I know what he's saying. We know lots of people at church—I might be able to name close to half of our six hundred members—well, not half but a lot of them, and I like just about everybody I know, but how many could you really call *friends*? I mean, if we had a really serious problem in the family, who would you call?"

"I'd call Pastor Tudway, of course. That's what he's there for."

Susan sighed. "Yes, I know, and he'd visit and pray for us and all that—but—I don't know—I can't really express it, but I do know what Jared's saying. The only person I know well enough at church to talk to about personal things is Betty in the library."

David shook his head. "I still don't get it. We've all got good Sunday school classes, Jared has teen activities, Deb has Kid's Stuff on Wednesday nights, you work in the library, I usher and serve on the board—what more do you want?"

Susan laughed and passed the fruit salad around the table again. "I don't want another job, that's for sure. But it seems like there should be something—I think I know exactly how Jared's feeling. I mean, I really like our Sunday school class—they're all neat people. But all I really know about them is what they think the prophecy in Daniel means or who can trace Paul's missionary journeys on a map." She finished with a smile.

David shook his head. "I hope you're not thinking we should have another program. No one wants to give up another night. Oh, speaking of that, Jared, I'm not sure I can make it to your soccer game Saturday. The pastor said this morning that the church board meeting may run late."

"Oh, David," Susan said, "you've got to—it's his first game of the season."

Jared shrugged. "Coach said I can't play anyway if I don't come up with the seventy dollars for the uniform and insurance. Mrs. Jones still owes me fifteen for mowing her lawn, but—"

The lines tightened around David's mouth, and the gray streaks in his black hair seemed suddenly whiter. "If Megacorp declares bankruptcy on that office building we started last month, soccer uniforms will be the least of our worries."

"I've got three dollars left from my birthday money from Uncle Clarence—you can use that." Debbie flipped her long blonde hair over her shoulder.

Susan grimaced, thinking that her salary as a school librarian simply wouldn't stretch any further. "Well, there's always the grocery money."

Jared groaned. "Oh, no—not baked beans again!"

The Flavells did have baked beans that week—twice. But even as much as Jared disliked beans it was worth it because Saturday he was off to his first game of the season. It didn't look, however, like his dad was going to get to see him play, because the church board meeting dragged on and on as they analyzed the report of the committee on church growth.

"So," Pastor Tudway summarized, "in spite of the fact that we take in new members regularly, most of them come to us by letter of transfer from other churches, or they've grown up in the church. We have very few joining by profession of faith. Overall, with people moving out, we're just keeping even, and when you consider the population growth of the city around us, that means we're losing ground."

Before he opened that problem up to further discussion he called for the report of the committee on body life ministry. That was equally gloomy as it focused on the need for more counseling. The needs of hurting people in their own congregation were not being met, let alone the needs in the community.

Dispiriting as the reports were, the discussion that followed was even worse.

"What we need is a real revival campaign. Not just one of those three-days-of-a-special-speaker things—I mean a solid ten days or two weeks of real old-fashioned preaching like we had when I was a kid. If people were really saved we wouldn't be having these problems." This contribution from

Boyd, a grade school principal, surprised those who didn't know him well. Boyd was barely into his middle thirties, but he held firmly to traditional values.

"I don't think you'll get people to come out for that—they're too busy. If they want to hear preaching, they'll watch the preachers on TV where they can sit in comfortable chairs and not have to put anything in the offering plate." Martin owned a small appliance store and made good use of the opportunities of media advertising.

"We don't need more old-fashioned stuff—we need more modern methods. Especially the music—excuse me, Chris," the speaker, the youngest member on the church board, nodded at the minister of music, "but we need more choruses and more modern music. Let's get some guitars in here."

Frank, the men's missionary president, had been sitting silently, but he couldn't take it any longer. "Now wait a minute—we're being too ingrown. The thing that's on my heart is missionaries. We need to look beyond ourselves and fulfill the Great Commission. The trouble is, no one comes to missionary meeting. There's a dying world out there, and nobody cares."

"Look, you've all got good points, but you're missing the most fundamental thing of all—prayer. We need more prayer, but less than ten percent of our people come to Wednesday night prayer meeting. We can't expect to grow or minister if we aren't praying." Ginny had spent twenty years as a public school teacher and as many teaching Sunday school. No one doubted the depth of her conviction.

Through all the sincere confusion one board member sat quietly in the back row, listening and thinking. Finally, George Carson raised his hand. "You know, I've got an idea we might consider. Two weeks ago I was in Denver visiting my sister. They've got a thing in their church that she's really big on —seems to be working great for them—they call it 'small groups.'"

Half of the heads in the room swiveled to look back at George. Most of them were frowning. Finally one person asked, "So what's a small group?"

THE SMALL GROUP REVOLUTION
—◆—

Do those questions sound familiar? Do you think that your church is good but could be better? Do you think you're doing a lot but should be doing more? Or are you doing too much but with too few results? Do you believe there should be a more effective way to function as Christ's Body on earth but don't know how to go about it?

Many church members across America are asking those questions—and finding the answers by joining what may be the most significant phenomenon in the Christian church in the late twentieth century—the small group revolution.

For the past twenty-five years individual churches have been incorporating small groups into their program structure. The quiet revolution has spread, and the results are exciting.

Our example is Christ. When Jesus started His ministry on earth, the first thing He did was to gather a small group. They came together with vastly different personalities and backgrounds. They ate together, they shared their struggles, they learned together, they prayed together, and they went out from their small group meetings to minister.

People today are finding their social, psychological, and spiritual needs met in the small group setting to a far more significant degree than has been possible in large group formats. Following the example of mega-churches, smaller churches are finding that they can do a far better job of discipling their members and reaching out to the unsaved around them when they instigate small group programs. In other words, through small groups, the whole church is growing together and becoming healthier.

CHAPTER TWO

Filling the Holes in Our Souls

*C*an I help you find a book?" Susan was in her favorite place in the church before services started—the library. She smiled at the young pregnant woman who was gazing at the shelves. "Are you new? I don't think we've met."

"Oh, well, not exactly new—we've been here several months. I just haven't got around very much. I'm Janice."

Susan smiled again, hoping to soothe the newcomer's uneasiness. "And I'm Susan. Where are you from?"

"Iowa, a small town. You wouldn't have heard of it."

"Well, welcome. What kind of a book were you looking for?"

Janice seemed embarrassed by the question. "Well," she dropped her voice, "something on loneliness, I guess. You see, all our family is back in Patton. And the church was really little, and we knew everybody, and . . . " Her voice trailed off, and she shrugged.

Before Susan could answer, a sandy-haired young man in his mid-twenties came in holding a bouncy three year old by the hand. Janice turned to them with relief. "Oh, this is my husband, Leon Croft, and daughter, Erin."

Susan said hi to Erin and shook hands with Leon. It wasn't until the family was out the door that she realized she hadn't found a book for Janice.

Susan went into her Sunday school class still thinking about the lost look in Janice's eyes but forgot about the Crofts when the teacher shared a prayer request with the class.

"I want you to pray for a fellow I've been golfing with—he's a lot better golfer than I am, but he has some real serious problems. He really opened up to me yesterday—said he's desperate. Seems he's had an alcohol problem for years. He's going to AA, but he's tried it before and failed. He said his wife says that if he doesn't make it this time she'll leave him. I invited him to church, but he says he wouldn't feel comfortable coming. I told him we'd pray for him."

"What's his name?" someone in the back asked.

"Al. Al and Karen. So let's remember them in prayer. And Martha in the hospital, and Joe and Alice on vacation—that they'll have a safe trip. Are there other needs?"

No one said anything, so the teacher called on David to pray, and then they turned to their study of the messianic psalms. This was one of Susan's favorite studies—she loved the psalms, and the ones that foretold the coming of Christ were especially beautiful, but today she found it hard to keep her mind on the lesson. She knew praying for someone was the most important thing she could do, but she wished she could do something else as well—put feet to her prayer, as the saying goes, for Al and Karen. And then she remembered the Crofts. Well, she hadn't found a book for them, but she could pray for them, too.

In the parking lot after church Debbie brought another need. "Mama, can I invite Lara over?"

"Who's Lara?"

"A girl in my Sunday school class. She doesn't come very often because her mom has to work late on Saturday nights —she's a waitress at the Red Lion."

Susan gulped, she had only put three potatoes in the oven, thinking she and Debbie could divide one. Well, she didn't really need a potato—or half a potato. "Sure, you can. I'll come along and talk to her mother."

Mitzi Montoya, Lara's mom, wore her black hair spiked on top and long in the back. Her gold loop earrings gleamed as brightly as her scarlet ice lipstick. "Well, sure—that's really sweet of you. Lara'd love to play with Debbie. She just loves Sunday school. I wish I could get her here more often—but some nights I don't get off work until one or two in the morning."

Susan got the address of the mobile home park where Lara and Mitzi lived and promised to take her home before the evening church service. The two girls skipped across the parking lot ahead of her, the sun shining on Debbie's blonde hair and Lara's dark curls. Susan sighed. Here was another family that needed prayer.

After dinner, when Debbie and her new friend had gone off to play and Jared had turned reluctantly to his homework, Susan poured another cup of coffee for herself and one for David. "Oh, beautiful quiet. I think this is my favorite moment of the week." She smiled at her husband. He smiled back, but the worried look didn't leave his eyes.

"So Megacorp filed bankruptcy?"

David nodded. "We got the notice yesterday."

"What will you do?"

David took a slow sip of coffee. "We've got a few stocks we can sell, but it won't be enough to pay the cement men and electrical subcontractors. Fortunately the plumbers hadn't done much yet, but we'll still owe them several thousand."

"And won't you get paid anything for your work? You'll have to pay your own men, too."

"Yep. That's the risks of the contracting business." He shook his head. "I don't know, there may be something when the building's sold. The hearing's next month."

Susan nodded. "I know. You feel so helpless when it's all beyond your own doing, and yet you get left holding the bag." She paused for a moment. "But you know, when I look at the problems all around us, I wouldn't trade with anyone." David nodded but didn't say anything, so she continued. "I was thinking this morning—there really are a lot of problems out there. I wish we could do more to help people—I mean, praying's important—but it's even hard to pray when you don't know what you should be praying for."

David pushed his cup over for a refill. "Well, there might be something we can do. I haven't told you about this new idea that came up at the church board meeting. It seems to be helping a lot of people."

WHY PEOPLE NEED SMALL GROUPS
◆

In preparing to write this book we interviewed several small groups and asked people, "Why did you join a small group?" Our theory was that people were lonely and looking for help with their problems. However, no one we talked with said, "I was lonely," or, "I had problems I couldn't handle." The majority of the answers had one major focus: "We wanted to make friends; we had moved away from our family back east; we didn't know anyone in the church . . ."

The fact is that people need people; we all need the love, friendship, and support of other human beings, whether we are happy or sad, whether we need help or want to give help. As Paul tells us in Romans 12:15, we should rejoice with those who rejoice and weep with those who weep.

We all need to connect and interact with other people. That used to happen naturally when people lived on farms or in small communities and had close families and small churches. But our population has grown, our urban social structures have become overwhelmingly large and impersonal, and our families have become the victims of more and more pressures, so people are finding themselves isolated and without the means to make the connections they long for.

We all have needs and hurts. None of us had a perfect childhood, none of us had perfect parents, none of us grew up without pain. That pain, usually from childhood but sometimes from later in life, leaves developmental holes in our souls. We have needs that must be ministered to, and we must minister to the needs of others.

As a culture we are experiencing spiritual and physical isolation. Family structures are crumbling while we pursue "the good life." Even Christians' lives are out of balance, and we experience pain and loneliness as a result. People are searching for connectedness but are unable to find it.

An applicable Bible verse is Psalm 68:6: "God sets the lonely in families." The small group is a family. It is a safe setting where people's social, spiritual, and psychological needs can be met. Nothing the world can offer compares with loving and being loved by like-minded believers.

The Holes in Our Souls from Social Needs
THE MEGA-SOCIETY

The sheer size of our social structures forces individuals into isolation. A friend from a small city in the Northwest told us recently that on a visit to the Los Angeles area she found herself coping with the frenzied freeway traffic by ignoring everything around her. "I suddenly realized that that might not be the safest approach to freeway driving—I probably should stay aware of what's going on in the lanes beside me," she said. But then she asked a key question. "Does this defense mechanism, which must be essential for most people to survive in large crowds, become so habitual that people just keep shutting everyone out even when they're looking for friends—even at church? Do people in big cities and big offices and big churches shut people out in order to cope?"

We answered a resounding yes. People are looking for connectedness to get them out of the isolation mode they have adopted, but they don't know how to shift gears and break through the walls they themselves have erected. And that doesn't apply only to people living in cities of four million or more—it's common for a mother of four children to shut out the noise of babbling voices until a child has to ask a question several times before he gets his mother's attention. It's entirely possible for two people to be together in a room yet be shutting each other out. And it's ironic that a person can be as isolated in a church of one hundred as in a church of one thousand. Small groups provide a structure to breach those walls of isolation and form needed connections.

People feel more human in small groups. Behavioral scientists have studied cases such as the widely publicized incident several years ago of Genevieve Wilson, who was stabbed twenty-seven times on a New York subway while sixty people looked on, ignoring her cries for help. The scientists discovered that although fears for personal safety were a factor in the apparent indifference, they were not controlling. People in such situations hold back because they are aware of the people around them: *If I mess up I'll look like a fool. Someone else will help—someone better at it than I am.*

A young air force officer who had studied that phenomenon knew better than just to shout for help when he was trying to rescue a drowning man. Instead, he looked one of the surrounding crowd in the eye and pointed at him. "Hey, you—help me!"

The teenager responded quickly because he thought, *He wants* me, *I've got to help.*

Then others in the circle of observers on the beach began to help because they had a role model to follow. "Come on, let's help him help."

In small groups we help each other rather than standing back and waiting for "someone trained to handle this" to step in.

In a big group we don't think other people are like ourselves. In a small group we see our commonality, and we're less defensive, less likely to see others as threats or obstacles. In a small group we see our roles more clearly and feel more confident. We see others as real people, so we can talk to them and relate to them because we realize, "They're just like me."

THE X-RATED SOCIETY

We are not only living in a society of overwhelming size; it is a society of overwhelming immorality. Ours is an X-rated society.

Popular television, movies, books, music—even the fashions one sees in the shopping mall or grocery store—are often openly and flagrantly immoral. We are surrounded by models of ungodliness, and it is becoming increasingly difficult to find models that exemplify the lifestyle Christians want to live.

Even those of us not attracted by sexual immorality will find our natural, carnal selves drawn to the glitter of materialistic society. We need to be bonded to Christian friends to help us obey the biblical injunction to "love not the world, neither the things that are in the world. If any man love the world, the love of the Father is not in him. For all that is in the world, the lust of the flesh, and the lust of the eyes, and the pride of life, is not of the Father, but is of the world" (1 John 2:15-16, NIV*).

The major functions of small groups are to provide (1) leaders who are role models and (2) a setting free from worldly standards.

THE "ME" GENERATION

Another side of the problem of people's getting lost in churches is those who are actually trying to hide. Some people want to be anonymous—especially those of the "me" generation. They are so involved in themselves and their own material goals that they don't want to make commitments, and they don't want to minister. Many are so self-centered that they don't even value their physical and spiritual families.

In *The Screwtape Letters,* C. S. Lewis says that Satan's goal is to make people want more and more things that satisfy less and less. The deceiver has made a great success of today's society. Tony Campolo tells about a time that as a mischievous youngster he and his friends went to the local Woolworth's and changed all the price tags around. That is what Satan has done to our world. He has put high value tags on things that will pass away and made things of eternal value look cheap. Possessions are valued more than people, frantic activity more than serenity, money more than morality,

New International Version.

quick thrills more than commitment, immediate gratification rather than true satisfaction, easy answers rather than truth.

People with those values can't be forced to join a small group or to interact with others at church, but we shouldn't make it too convenient for them to sidestep commitment. You can't force people—but you can make attractive opportunities available to them.

THE BREAKDOWN OF FAMILIES

Just as the size, immorality, and materialism of society place enormous pressures on individuals, so those factors also create pressure within families. One of the most severe is the pressure to succeed. In modern families children are often pushed to be in honors classes in school, to do well in sports, and to take gymnastics or ballet as well as music lessons outside of school. And Christian families have the increased pressure of church programs as well. Small groups can help ease the pressures by providing a balanced perspective in an atmosphere where the focus is on emotional bonding rather than on social achievement.

Geographical separation is another factor contributing to family breakdown today. Even stable nuclear families need extended family, but very few have that luxury today because of geographic restrictions. Allen Doran grew up in a middle-class family on Long Island, and his family was very close. He visited his grandparents every weekend—which he hated as a kid, because everybody just sat around and talked. But now, from the perspective of many years and thousands of miles, he looks back at those family gatherings with all the aunts and uncles and cousins and realizes how much has been lost. His children don't have extended family around them in California.

Families seldom gather together anymore—it's even difficult within the nuclear family—and so we are finding less intimate bonding in families and more dysfunction. There is less leadership as husbands abdicate their role and wives are frustrated by husbands who don't seem to care. One family is a typical example: the father works for an Alaskan oil company and is gone one week, home one week, gone one week. The wife performs the traditional role functions of both mother and father. At first Dr. Doran was shocked when the wife seemed to accept this as normal; but then he realized that it isn't too different from what really goes on in most families —it's just that most fathers aren't so visibly far away. With this lack of family structure, people everywhere are starved for emotional bonding but without a clue as to how to get it. They look to the church, but most churches don't fill that need.

Time and space don't permit a full development here of all the pressures on families today—divorce, single parenting, drugs, abortion, and so on. But we don't really need an in-depth discussion of those things—they are all too familiar to us. We all know the pressures we face; what we really need is answers.

Small groups are surrogate families and can significantly help us cope with the pressures around us. They can provide a safe enclosure for the nuclear family—a buffer zone between the family and the world. Many families describe their small group as a sanctuary. They can go out into the world, then come back to a safe place to assimilate their experiences in the company of loving friends.

The Holes in Our Souls from Spiritual Needs

Just as none of us grew up in a perfect family, so also none of us, even those who were raised in a Christian environment, grew up in a perfect church. Even if we had, we were born with original sin, so we will have spiritual needs as long as we're in this world. We all need to keep growing in the Lord—even those who have been Christians for sixty years —and small groups provide a wonderful atmosphere for spiritual growth, both as we grow ourselves and as we strengthen each other in the Lord.

The ultimate purpose of life is to know and love God and to glorify Him. Small groups function as a means of grace in striving for this goal as we grow together through the shared experiences of others. The best place to grow in the Body of Christ is in a situation where you can function freely using your own gifts and talents in vital relationships with other believers. In small groups you can break down walls, learn to accept others who are different from you, and learn to be vulnerable in an accepting atmosphere.

Paul Meier uses his own spiritual goals as an illustration. Every morning he dedicates his day to becoming more like Christ and serving Him. His key scripture is Matthew 6:33-34: "Seek first His kingdom and His righteousness; and all these things shall be added to you. Therefore do not be anxious about tomorrow; for tomorrow will care for itself. Each day has enough trouble of its own." His small group helps him reach those goals by helping him keep life in perspective; it helps him refocus on what's important and on finding solutions that work to meet his emotional needs.

Just as the goal of the individual is to become a mature Christian, so the goal of the church is to produce mature Christians "until we all attain to the unity of the faith, and of the knowledge of the Son of God, to a mature man, to the measure of the stature which belongs to the fulness of Christ" (Eph. 4:13).

Nothing succeeds like success, and nothing promotes growth like growing. In other words, we need to check our growth. Just as a pediatrician regularly checks an infant's weight, length, and development, we need to measure our spiritual growth to be sure that we are no longer children, tossed to and fro and carried about with every wind of doctrine, gullible to crafty rogues and deceitful schemes. We should be speaking the truth in love so that we fully grow in Christ (Eph. 4:14-15).

Christians need to be producing the fruit of the Holy Spirit: love, joy, peace, longsuffering, kindness, goodness, faithfulness, gentleness, and self-control. Small groups help us produce this fruit. The Holy Spirit is the gardener, we are the seed, and the small group is the garden in which we grow. It is important to understand the small group in that light—it is not just an activity, not just another program. It is a structure for ministry, a garden for growth.

The Holes in Our Souls from Psychological Needs

One of our most basic needs is to bond to other people. Most psychologists believe that until the age of eighteen months we all think we're part of our mothers. Once we discover that we are separate people, we can begin forming connections to other people. In a healthy person this bonding process continues throughout life: in the nuclear family, in the extended family, in school friendships and business associations, in marriage and a new nuclear family, and in church relationships. But because of childhood pain and pressures of society, bonding is more difficult today than ever before, and people are experiencing emotional voids in their lives when it does not happen. Although bonding is one of the biggest needs among both Christians and non-Christians, people don't know how to achieve it.

This need for bonding, which the Flavell family was expressing without knowing it, is equally important whether one is in the pulpit or the pew. Dr. Doran had a friend who was a dynamic pastor. The man was brilliant and magnetic. He started a church with six couples and built it to a congregation of two thousand people. But he had no bonding with the people in his church or his family—no emotional sharing on an intimate basis. When his church reached the two thousand-member peak he asked, "Is this all there is?"

In spite of his administrative and material success, that man felt like a failure. A two-thousand-member mega-church couldn't fill the emotional void in his soul because he wasn't bonded to individuals.

Besides bonding to one another, we need to be bonded to God. Bonding to God is actually an extension of earthly bonding, because we bond to God by being bonded to each other. On the sixth day of creation, God made man and woman in His own image so that they could join together and to Him. And God declared that to be "very good." To achieve bonding is to find God's balance for your life.

Intimacy with God is strengthened by trusting Him, by prayer, by meditation on Scripture, and by listening to Him —all of which are functions of the small group. The small group can help you develop an attitude of "thinking God." Bonding to God entails thinking about Him, His nature, His teachings, and His exciting future plans for you.

In true bonding we love and are loved just as we love Christ and He loves us. We find our true worth as we minister in the lives of other people. This is the small group.

HOW SMALL GROUPS MET THEIR NEEDS
◆

We asked dozens of people—some who had been in small groups for as long as fifteen years, some who had just decided to join and were looking forward to attending their first meeting—"Why did you decide to join a small group?" Perhaps some of their answers will mirror your own feelings.

"I wanted to be with people who wanted the same things out of life as I do—people who want God" was one of the most common answers. People talked about how secular the conversations were in their workplace, how seldom they saw their neighbors—and then only to talk about leaf or snow removal or a third neighbor's cat killing small trees—and how much they longed to be able to talk about God in their lives.

"I grew up in a small town in Kansas. I knew everybody —they were all friendly. As a teenager if I did anything wrong, people knew my family and I was accountable. Here I am in a city of four million—how do I relate to four million people? Who cares if I'm getting sloppy in my Christian life—just as long as I don't run any red lights? A small group is how you make small towns." Even in small towns, we reminded this harried business executive, people need relationships where they are noticed and accountable.

Brad, an earnest young man with wide, dark eyes and curly black hair, gave us something of an embarrassed smile. "Well, I know this makes me sound shallow and lacking in commitment, but I've been church hopping ever since I got out of college five years ago. I suppose it *is* a form of lack of commitment—at least uncommittedness—but it's *not* a lack of desire to make a commitment to the Body of Christ. I'm looking for a place where I can put down real spiritual roots." He paused to flash a smile of joy quite unlike his earlier expression. "I'm getting married in six months, and I want a real church home where we can build our marriage and raise kids. But until I found this small group thing, nothing filled the bill of what I—really we, because Jenny's been looking, too—needed. I think we've found it now—the place God wants us to be."

A comfortable-looking woman approaching the grandmother stage overheard our conversation. "Hi, I'm Edith—do you mind if I join in?"

We welcomed her and explained we were looking for a range of stories.

"Well, I just wanted to tell Brad that five years of church hopping is nothing. I've been stuck in that trap for nigh unto ten years now. I'd settle in anywhere just to be settled. I want friends—even though the preacher and I have some differences—but Fred, my husband, he can't agree with anything from any pulpit, it seems. So imagine my surprise when he really settled into a small group. I think maybe it's because the leader isn't dogmatic, or because we're all laymen, or maybe because Fred can always enter into the discussion if he wants to—I don't know what it is, but we've finally found a place to belong, and I can't tell you how happy I am!"

Two young women in their mid-thirties told us how their small groups ministered to people beyond their immediate families. "My small group is a witness to my non-Christian friends. I told them that my group brought in meals when I was sick after Janell's birth," one said, smiling at the tiny girl pulling on her hand. "My friends were really impressed to see Christianity in action."

"And my small group ministers indirectly to my family and friends all around the country," Rebecca added. "They call and say, 'Will you have your small group pray for me?'"

The discussion went on, expressed in terms as various as the personalities God has created, but some of the most repeated themes, ones that seemed to go directly to the heart of the matter, were the briefest: "Hearing people talk about their lives encourages me." "We're looking for Christian friends." "I want to belong."

CHAPTER THREE

Producing a Mature Church

*D*avid Flavell looked at the stack of bills on his desk and shook his head. It wasn't of much use to *his* creditors that the bankruptcy judge had declared him a bona fide creditor and said he would get a portion of the proceeds when Megacorp's assets were sold. Even a judge's promise wouldn't pay his phone, gas, and electricity bills.

"David, you're going to be late for the church board meeting." Susan's voice reached him through his half-closed office door. For once he was glad for an excuse to leave his desk—there wasn't anything he could do there anyway.

"'Bye, Deb, Jared—you'll probably be in bed by the time I get back. See you tomorrow." David waved to his kids.

Susan kissed him good-bye. "I'll wait up."

All the way to church David worried about those bills. Maybe he should resign from the church board—what place did he have deciding on church business when his own was in such chaos? But if he resigned he'd have to explain, and even though Christians *say* material success isn't what's important, it's still how people keep score. Feeling like a failure was bad enough—having to admit it publicly was something else. No, he'd just hold his head up and keep on. At least Susan's library job kept food on the table. But both of the kids needed new shoes.

The board meeting provided a much-needed shift for David's thinking. It was refreshing to focus on the needs of the church instead of his own problems.

And the format of the board meeting was relaxing, too. Pastor Tudway explained that in response to George Carson's comments at the last meeting regarding the successful ministry of the church in Denver he had asked George to get more information. "I think we all agree that we're doing a lot of things right. But we also have a vague feeling that we should be doing more. You'll recall, though, that at our last meeting we couldn't agree on what we needed to do. George has a videotape for us that explains some of the biblical principles his sister's church has followed in developing their ministry. Let's see what we can learn that might be helpful to our situation. George, you ready to start it for us?"

David took out his pen and sketched on the pad in front of him as the teacher on the television screen explained what the Bible says makes a successful church, or how God measures a church. From 1 Corinthians 13:13; Ephesians 1:15-18; Colossians 1:3-5; 1 Thessalonians 1:2-3; and 2 Thessalonians 1:3-4 he drew the biblical principle of the measure of a church: faith, hope, and love.

David listed the three words on his notepad and doodled stars and boxes around them as he wondered how to produce more of those qualities in their church, and for a while his thoughts drifted off, hoping that the solution wouldn't be anything expensive such as a building program or a new missions project, because it would be so embarrassing not to be able to contribute.

His attention jerked back to the videoscreen as he heard the teacher ask, "Now, what kind of experiences do Christians need to become mature in Jesus Christ? What is going to produce a dynamic *faith*? What is going to produce *hope*? What is going to produce *love*?"

And as he went on to list the three vital experiences that produce a mature church, David listed them on his paper:

1. Learning experiences with the Word of God.
2. Relational experiences with one another and with God.
3. Witnessing experiences with non-Christians.

Pastor Tudway clicked off the videotape.* "This is what we've got to decide. Are we at Bethany Bible Church providing all three of those experiences for our people? What about the three legs—doctrine, fellowship, and evangelism?

"I want us to look at our balance. I'm especially concerned about our fellowship leg, but I want to know what you think. And another question—how can we best structure our church to provide these experiences for our people to grow together?

"I've spent a lot of time with George this past week hearing about the small group he visited—it sounds great, but before we propose anything new, we need to see where we are. I've got a survey form here. I want each of you to take this home and analyze the emphasis of our church. Changes that

* Much of the material in this chapter is taken from a videotape series by Gene Getz titled Sharpening the Focus of the Church, available from the Center for Church Renewal, 200 Chisolm Place, Suite 228, Plano TX 75075.

need to be made in the pulpit I'm willing to make, but changes in the daily lives of our people and in the fellowship and evangelism areas we may need to restructure for—something like this small group program George keeps bringing up. Let's take a look at it."

WHY CHURCHES NEED SMALL GROUPS

——♦——

A healthy church must stand firm on all three legs of its biblical purpose: learning from God's Word and praising God together in corporate worship (doctrine); sharing and loving one another (fellowship); and reaching out to the unsaved in the strength that the first two activities produce (evangelism).

In a mature church, balance among those legs is key. Problems can develop when only one is emphasized. Overemphasis on Bible teaching can produce cognitive Christianity and spiritual pride; focusing only on fellowship can produce people who rely on feelings and fluctuate up and down emotionally; overstressing evangelism leaves people starving for solid, consistent Bible teaching and deep relationships.

Likewise, emphasizing only two of the three experiences can be dangerous. For example, an emphasis on Bible teaching and fellowship but not evangelism produces churches that neglect outreach and become like dammed up rivers. Churches need the fresh flow of new life to keep maturing. Relational Christianity and evangelism can produce lots of fresh green sprouts, but without solidly rooted Bible teaching no branches will be strong enough to support the new growth. And as important as evangelism and Bible teaching are, without fellowship, relationships become superficial.

Whatever the situation of your local church—whether you're growing rapidly or not growing at all—you can benefit from small group fellowships, because each situation produces its own problems. A nongrowing or slowly growing church can stagnate. Its people need to branch out so they can produce fruit. On the other hand, in a rapidly growing church the growth is often shallow, requiring the need for deeper roots. Even if the growth is accompanied by depth, the sheer numbers make it likely that many people will be overlooked and their needs unmet.

John Stott wrote in an article on church renewal, "Every healthy local church will have not only a united service of dignity on the Lord's day, but also it will divide the congregation into fellowship groups which meet in each other's homes during the week. We need both, we must not choose between them."[1]

Maturing Through Corporate Worship

One of the most beautiful metaphors the New Testament uses to describe the church is the body. In Ephesians 4 Paul describes God's process for bringing a church to maturity: "Building up of the body of Christ; until we all attain to the unity of the faith . . . being fitted and held together by that which every joint supplies, according to the proper working of each individual part, causes the growth of the body for the building up of itself in love" (vv. 12-16).

Corporate worship is essential if the Body is to grow together. We cannot truly worship together if we are each our own little island, relating to God in our own way. Unity must be achieved in two directions: horizontally with one another, and vertically with God. Coming together as a congregation bonded through small group experiences will bring unity to the church. In this way small groups support whole-church worship.

It is important to understand the corporate nature of most of the biblical injunctions because the overall tone of Scripture is corporate: corporate prayer, corporate evangelism, corporate ministry. In our Western culture we personalize the second person pronoun in Scripture, but in the original manuscripts of Scripture *you* is almost always a plural pronoun.

In John 17, Christ's prayer for believers is "that they may all be one." Oneness can be achieved through worshiping together because true worship means focusing on God rather than on ourselves. We must never become so focused on our needs and problems that we neglect worship and praise. Paul emphasizes the importance of corporate worship in Hebrews 13:15: "Through Jesus, therefore, let us continually offer to God a sacrifice of praise—the fruit of lips that confess his name" (NIV). And in Ephesians 5:19-20, "Speak to one another with psalms, hymns and spiritual songs. Sing and make music in your heart to the Lord, always giving thanks to God the Father for everything, in the name of our Lord Jesus Christ" (NIV).

In *Praying for One Another* Gene Getz quotes numerous selections from the Psalms to show what they say about prayer and praise. We quote two here.

> *When* to Praise God
> I will extol the Lord at all times; his praise will always be on my lips. . . . But I will sing of your strength, in the morning I will sing of your love. . . . Praise be to his glorious name forever; may the whole earth be filled with his glory. Amen and Amen. . . . Every day I will praise you and extol your name for ever and ever. (Psalms 34:1; 59:16; 72:19; 145:2, NIV)

> *Where* to Praise God
> I will praise you in the presence of your saints. . . . I will praise you, O Lord, among the nations; I will sing of you among the peoples. . . . Praise the Lord. Praise God in his sanctuary; praise him in his mighty heavens. (Psalms 52:9; 57:9; 150:1, NIV)

In *Praying the Psalms* Thomas Merton says that "in the Psalms, we drink divine praise at its pure source . . . these are the songs of the whole Church, the very expression of her deepest inner life." Merton says that when the church sings the psalms together "she is singing of her knowledge of God, of her union with Him." In singing together about God we are "singing the wedding hymn of our union with God in Christ."[2]

Worship, the edification of the Body of Christ, must not be left undone. But always we must remember that in worship, as in the other legs of a healthy church, the key is not either-or but both-and. The Christians in Jerusalem had dynamic fellowship with God *and* with one another, *and* they reached out to others in missionary efforts.

Maturing Through Fellowship

We have focused on Paul's analogy of the church as a body in our discussion of corporate worship, but the apostle uses another analogy for the church in Romans when he says, "Be devoted to one another in brotherly love" (12:10). Here we have the metaphor of a family. We are all brothers and sisters in God's family. The analogy works perfectly for those who grew up in healthy, loving families of origin. When such a person is invited to become part of God's family, he or she can respond readily.

But a person who grew up in a home void of love, security, and acceptance will probably come into God's family with struggles. He will still feel that no one cares for him.

God designed the human family to be a model of His family, and He designed the Body of Christ to function as parents to people who didn't grow up in healthy families. Because of its smaller size and its bonding function, the small group is especially well suited for reparenting people, for bringing them into the family of God and teaching them how to love, and for making them feel comfortable and wanted.

Those from dysfunctional families, however, are not the only ones who need the small group experience. Individuals from healthy families of origin need fellowship with other Christians because it is a spiritual necessity. The quality of our relationship with God is determined by the quality of our relationships with one another. Even Jesus needed small group fellowship—quiet times of communicating with His disciples.

It is in the small group that we can best minister to one another. The phrase "one another" is used more than sixty times in the New Testament. Paul alone uses it more than forty times in conjunction with exhortations—outlining what we are to do for one another. Gene Getz's One Another books summarize Paul's admonitions on how to grow together into Christian maturity.[3] He develops the scriptural principle that Christians should be involved in each other's lives. They should be concerned about each other and growing together to strengthen the whole Body and glorify God.

Maturing Through Evangelism

Small groups can be an extremely effective arm of evangelism for the church. First, they can provide opportunities for people to become Christians. It is not unusual for people to join a small group simply because they are looking for friends; when they find friends, they find Christ as well. Nor is it unusual for people to join a small group thinking they are Christians, then, through the discipling process of the group, discover that they didn't really know what Christianity was after all.

One of the most effective ways for small groups to evangelize is seen in the biblical injunction that "they will know we are Christians by our love." The small group should exemplify love in action so that non-Christians are drawn to it. In His high priestly prayer in John 17, Christ's primary concern for His church is that it exhibit a visible unity—a oneness that reveals the very essence of the gospel. Satan's strategy throughout church history has been to destroy unity in the Body of Christ. If the enemy can destroy unity, he will have destroyed the most powerful means of communicating to a lost world the fact that Jesus Christ is God.

However, it is unwise for the small group to engage in confrontational evangelistic efforts until the members are thoroughly bonded—which may take as long as two years. Then they can reach out to others from the strength of their unity. Coming together as a community of believers must be the primary function of a small group. Too much evangelism at first can hinder bonding within the group. A constant flow of visitors to the group will prevent in-depth sharing.

If a group is truly fulfilling its function of bonding and living out Christian love, evangelism will be a natural outgrowth. As a group matures, having a "warm spiritual time" will not be enough; believers will naturally begin to reach out to others.

Many of the small groups in Gene Getz's church function as effective evangelistic tools when members bring non-Christian spouses or friends to meetings—just to expose them to vital Christian love. One small group recently participated in a unique outreach effort to plant small groups in another church about 250 miles away. The pastor from a small struggling church in Siloam Springs had visited the Center for Church Renewal looking for help for his congregation. He saw small groups in action and said, "This is what we need."

The established small group caught the vision of helping their Christian brothers and sisters. They wrote to them, prayed for them, sent them material from their own church. But none of it seemed to be enough. Finally, one of their quietest members suggested, "Let's go *show* them how it's done." And fifteen people from that small group made the five-hour drive to Siloam Springs. "Mostly we went to encourage them—to show them we care," one member said. They also conducted a model small group for them and held a question and answer session.

"I'm sure we helped them. We've had enthusiastic reports of their new program since we got back," their leaders said. "But it was also a great boost to our own small group. We've been more open to each other's needs since we went out to minister."

Some small groups are involved in special evangelistic and outreach projects, such as supporting specific missionaries, both financially and in prayer, inner-city missions, visitor follow-up, and so on. This is an important aspect of small group ministry in that it develops a sense of ownership often not felt in the church at large. However, such efforts must have central church coordination to avoid overlapping efforts and conflict of interests.

MEASURING YOUR OWN CHURCH

◆

As you look at your own church, apply God's measuring rod of faith, hope, and love to it. Could Paul say of you as he said of the Thessalonians, "We give thanks to God always for all of you . . . constantly bearing in mind your work of *faith* and labor of *love* and steadfastness of *hope* in our Lord Jesus Christ" (1 Thess. 1:3; italics added)? Faith is measurable by works. Love can be measured by labor, and hope by steadfastness. How do you measure up? When a body of believers looks in a mirror it should see the image of Jesus Christ reflected. They should see patience, kindness, self-control, purity, humility, unselfishness. If Paul sat down today to write a letter to your church, what would he thank God for?

Those were the questions David Flavell was wrestling with late that night when he returned to his desk. For once, he was unaware of the stack of unpaid bills, for he was struggling to apply God's measure to his church as he filled out the survey from Pastor Tudway.

We invite you to apply this evaluation scale to your church to determine which of the three legs are emphasized in your body and which need more development. Does your church emphasize all three? Where are you strongest? Where are you weak? How well are the three experiences balanced? Is your church weak in an area that could be strengthened by small groups? Has your church tried a small group approach that was less than successful? If so, do you see how small groups might be approached again in a new light?

PERSONAL PROJECT
———◆———

How would you categorize your church in terms of emphasis? The following evaluation scale will help you answer that question.

1. How do the forms and structures of my church allow for a balance between learning the Word of God, having relational experiences with one another and with God, and sharing Christ with others?

   Unsatisfactory   1   2   3   4   5   Satisfactory

2. Is the Word of God taught clearly and regularly?

   Unsatisfactory   1   2   3   4   5   Satisfactory

3. Is the Word of God taught with variety—verse by verse, topical studies, biographical studies, and so on?

   Unsatisfactory   1   2   3   4   5   Satisfactory

4. Is there a balance between teaching from the Old Testament and the New Testament?

   Unsatisfactory   1   2   3   4   5   Satisfactory

5. Is the Word of God applied to twentieth-century life and practice?

   Unsatisfactory   1   2   3   4   5   Satisfactory

6. Am I learning how to study the Word of God on my own?

   Unsatisfactory   1   2   3   4   5   Satisfactory

7. Do our structures allow for relationships with God to grow naturally out of relationships with people?

   Unsatisfactory   1   2   3   4   5   Satisfactory

8. Do our structures and approaches allow for Communion to be a meaningful experience, involving deep relationships with people?

   Unsatisfactory   1   2   3   4   5   Satisfactory

9. Is prayer vital and dynamic, based on an awareness of human needs in the body?

   Unsatisfactory   1   2   3   4   5   Satisfactory

10. Is giving spontaneous, regular, and joyful in the context of meeting the needs of people?

    Unsatisfactory   1   2   3   4   5   Satisfactory

11. Does our music represent a balance between songs and hymns that teach and admonish one another and those that exalt and glorify God? Do we have the freedom to use music that is expressed in various ways, or do we only use music that we are culturally conditioned to accept and appreciate?

    Unsatisfactory   1   2   3   4   5   Satisfactory

12. Do our structures allow opportunities to share Christ with others? Are we too busy to share Christ and build bridges with non-Christians?

Unsatisfactory 1   2   3   4   5   Satisfactory

13. Do we have time to relate to members of the Body of Christ outside of the church building—in our homes, in recreational settings, and in the context of informality? Or are our relationships with people limited to attending meetings together?

Unsatisfactory 1   2   3   4   5   Satisfactory

14. Do we have time to be with our families? Do church structures compete with our family life?

Unsatisfactory 1   2   3   4   5   Satisfactory

CHAPTER FOUR

Laying the Groundwork 1: Leadership

*S*usan Flavell punched and pulled at the lump of soft brown bread dough. It was just getting to the elastic, satiny stage that was fun to knead. Susan enjoyed baking bread for her family and giving fresh-baked loaves to her friends. It would be nice, though, she thought, not to *have* to bake bread every week—especially on days like this when David wanted her to go to a meeting at church, and she had three story hour preparations to do for Monday. *Well, I could take a loaf of bread for a visual with "The Little Red Hen."* Too bad the classes for older children weren't so easy.

When the phone rang she hooked it over her shoulder, so she could talk and keep working. "Uncle Clarence! How are you? . . . You sound tired. . . . When can you come see us? The kids miss you . . . " They talked for a while, then Susan hung up the phone with a sigh. She hated having her only relative live six hundred miles away, and he'd sounded so lonesome since his wife died last year.

David came in and gave Susan a quick kiss on the cheek. She smiled and dabbed a spot of flour on the end of his nose. He asked, "Is this going to be out of the oven in time for you to go to the renewal meeting with me?"

Susan plunked the bread dough into a greased mixing bowl to rise. "David, I'm so tired, and I've still got all that ironing to do."

David nodded and put his arm around his wife. "I know —this disaster in my business has meant an awful lot of extra work for you. But Pastor Tudway emphasized the importance of elders coming as couples. And you were the one who said a few weeks ago we needed more fellowship and a better way to minister to others."

Susan untied her apron. "Ministering to you and the kids is about all I can cope with at the minute, but I'll go with you. Debbie can put this in the pans when it's ready. Who did you say the speaker is?"

"Eric Lions. He's from the Church Support Center in Denver. When the board decided we should really get serious about starting a small group program, Pastor Tudway arranged for him to come and help us get organized."

A short time later Susan was sitting in a pew at church, but her mind was still back home on her bread. *Maybe I should call Deb and remind her to check it*—then her attention was caught by the solid-looking man in the crisp blue linen shirt Pastor Tudway had just introduced. "I am delighted with the groundwork you've done here before I came," Eric Lions said. "You've started at exactly the right place—examining the scriptural principles of how God measures a church and then evaluating your own structure to see if you have a good balance in your body."

Susan nodded. She had seen the form David filled out, and they had discussed many of the questions together. But she hadn't realized she was letting herself in for such a big project. Eric continued. "I've been delighted with the results of that survey. You have a really good church here—a church that teaches the Bible and cares about people. That's why I'm so pleased to help you find a way to improve the effectiveness of your ministry through organizing small groups.

"And I'm delighted to see your wholehearted support of this project, Pastor." The speaker turned to Pastor Tudway, who nodded at him. "In many situations, the movement for renewal comes from the people and is resisted by pastors. Of course, anything new can be a threat. And I think liberal pastors are especially threatened—because when you have small groups of people studying the Word and ministering to each other, you'll find your congregation moving back to basics. Some leaders don't want that.

"And then, there are some insecure leaders who don't want any of the leadership to get out of their control. We at the Church Support Center have helped congregations who have leadership problems like that, but it's a joy to be here at Bethany Bible where you are all starting off in unity. The program will have the maximum effectiveness if your pastor is sold on it and involved himself—some congregations have to settle for simply having their pastor's permission."

The speaker turned to the staff sitting down front to his right. "This is probably as good a time as any to tell you the good news and the bad news for the church staff about small groups. As you all know, there is a great deal of—shall we call it social pressure?—on senior pastors and staff members and their wives and families to be perfect—to be dressed perfectly but not expensively, to keep a perfect house but not spend too much time on it, to attend every church service and activity, and have time for a well-rounded life, too!" Every head on the first two rows was nodding, especially those of the wives. No one meant to burden their pastoral staff and families with all that—but it seemed to be an inescapable fact of life.

Eric smiled at the nodding heads. "The good news is that because each small group has its own leader—lay pastor, if you will—this pressure is dispelled from the senior pastor and his staff. People have many leaders to focus on, and the demands are lessened because they are diffused."

Susan frowned at that. He hadn't said yet that elders were to take the leadership roles, but she could see it coming —did that mean she was supposed to be *encouraged* because some of that pressure was going to be transferred to her? She had an idea that if she listened very hard she would hear the voice of Christ asking, "Are you willing to bear this for Me?" But she didn't want to listen.

Eric Lions continued. "Another pressure you're all aware of is the time pressure of trying to meet the needs of a congregation of several hundred people. Here there's good news, too. The small group structure distributes much of this responsibility to lay pastors, who report to the staff pastors. Small group leaders and members visit hospitals, take food to those who are sick, and comfort the bereaved—thereby helping to relieve some of that pressure from your staff. This is not only sensible and efficient, but it's also scriptural. I'll point you to just one example, from the eighteenth chapter of Exodus, that of Moses and his father-in-law. When Jethro saw Moses sitting day and night attending to the needs of the people, he said, 'What do you think you're doing?'

"'The people come to me, and I tell them God's laws, and I judge between them,' Moses said.

"And Jethro said, 'This is no good. You'll wear yourself out. Teach the people God's laws, and appoint men to judge the people, rulers of thousands and rulers of hundreds and rulers of fifties and rulers of tens.'"

Then Eric cleared his throat, turned to look at Pastor Tudway behind him, and continued. "I warned you that there was bad news, too. An effective small group program will take a great deal more in administrative time and leadership training time than a traditional style church program. Instead of a staff of five to ten to oversee, now you'll have a staff of twenty-five to fifty."

"And just those five can be pretty unruly, let me tell you," Pastor Tudway inserted good-naturedly.

Eric laughed with the others, then went on. "But the news gets worse. You'll also have more call for counseling, Pastor, because when people bond, their needs will be uncovered. Problems that people have kept bottled up behind a set smile every Sunday morning for years will surface in the small group. I can guarantee that the more effective you are, the more people problems you'll have."

For the first time Susan nodded. Somehow, the bad news was the most attractive part of the program. She thought of Al and his alcohol problem—he had visited Sunday school once but hadn't been back in the past three weeks. She hoped Karen hadn't carried out her threat to leave him. And Debbie had had such a good time with her new friend, Lara, that time she had come over, but they hadn't seen her since. And—what was her name?—that new lady who was about to have a baby—what had become of that family?

Yes, it would be worth committing some of her already-squeezed time and energy to a program that could really help people.

Eric Lions went on to discuss the process of leadership selection and training and the logistics of small group meetings, especially focusing on ideas for incorporating such a program into Bethany Bible's traditional structure. Even though he had charts, films, and printed material to make his explanation clear, Susan wasn't really following it. She looked at the people around her—the elders, deacons and stewards, church board members and Sunday school teachers who had been invited to this informational meeting—did those people have problems? They all looked as if they knew the Bible forward and backward. Did they need small groups too?

Then she looked at her hands folded in her lap. She flicked a bit of bread dough from under a finger nail. Did her family need a small group? Did *she* need one? She remembered Jared's complaint that he didn't have any real friends at church—just acquaintances. She had been thinking of the small group as a means to minister to others. Did she and her family need one to minister to them?

BEHIND THE SCENES

♦

Any successful program takes weeks—even months—of careful preparation before its public launch. With a mixture of apprehension and eagerness, the staff and church board of Bethany Bible Church voted to launch a small group program. Eric Lions's visit was the catalyst for moving them from the exploration stage into beginning the actual work.[1] But there are other ways to lay the groundwork also.

It is absolutely necessary for the leadership of your church to be sold on the program. A good way to develop this unity is to provide an in-depth study for church leaders and board members by using a book or other tool.[2] From the first it is important to be up-front about the demands of a small group ministry. Everyone involved needs to know that there will be lots of work. Small groups require more leaders than traditional structures do; they produce more variables in your mix of people, and more problems emerge. Staff and leaders need to know it is not an easy road, but it does accomplish real ministry.

The congregation also needs to be prepared. A series of sermons on the mission of the church based on the book of Acts might help people see what they're doing right and where they need to make improvements in the life of their church and in their own lives.

While these dynamics of change are at work in your church, you can be laying the foundation of success by selecting and training your leaders.

CHOOSING LEADERS
◆

When you launch your small group ministry, leaders should be hand-picked. A good place to start is with your elders. Hopefully they are mature people who have proved their leadership capabilities. Later, as the program grows, new leaders will emerge from the small groups, and the elders can shepherd the small group leaders. But initially it is essential that the pastor have leaders he can rely on.

If you ask someone to lead, he will be honored. The knowledge that "my pastor chose me" is a good motivator. But the pastor must also be willing to say "no, thank you" when inappropriate candidates volunteer for leadership positions.

It is also important to pick leaders who are loyal to the growth of the local church and who have no desire to ride their hobbyhorses off on doctrinal tangents.

A leader must be a mature Christian who fits the biblical qualifications listed in Titus 2:2: sober, high-principled, temperate, sound in faith, in love, and in endurance; and those in 1 Timothy 3: above reproach, morally pure, temperate, hospitable, a good teacher, not given to drink or a brawler but of forbearing disposition, and no lover of money. He must be one who manages his own household well and wins obedience from his children, as well as a man of the highest principles. And he must be a servant. Finally, leaders should be committed to the church financially. They must be good models to the people to whom they will be ministering.

Some churches have found it helpful to have couples as leaders. One leader said, "My wife is key to my being a leader. She thinks of all the things I'd miss—such as taking food to a couple in our group the day they moved into a new house. A big part of the fun is leading our group together —it's a good way for us to grow together as a couple. And because so many marriages today are troubled, it's important that the leadership couple be a good role model."

Leaders of small groups in Gene Getz's church are given a number of weeks of leadership training. That degree of intensity is important because their leaders have the authority to function as pastors. They select the materials for their group to study, they baptize people, they serve Communion, and they counsel other couples. Of course each local church will want to make such decisions for itself.

There are three areas in which a man needs to be trained and approved before serving as a small group leader. The areas are: character, ministry and leadership skills, and knowledge. The following guidelines are designed to help evaluate potential leaders in these areas.

EVALUATION FOR A SMALL GROUP LEADER

CHARACTER

Relationship with God
1. Does he spend regular time in prayer?
2. Does he spend regular time in the Word?

3. Is he a mature believer? (In answering this question, reflect on the fruit of the Spirit [Gal. 5] and the qualities of an elder [1 Tim. 3; Titus 1].)

Relationships in His Family
1. Does he love his wife as Christ loved the church? Is his marriage solid?
2. Does he have his children in control? Is his family strong?

Relationships in the Church
1. Is he committed to the church? to the small group?
2. Does he show his commitment financially?
3. Is he willing to be held accountable?

Relationships in the World
1. Does he have a good reputation in the business community? in his workplace?
2. Is he financially responsible?
3. Does he share his faith?

MINISTRY AND LEADERSHIP SKILLS

Administrative
1. Can he manage himself and others?
2. Can he lead effectively?

Small Group Dynamics
1. Can he lead a good discussion about a biblical passage?
2. Can he facilitate relationships in a group?

Personal Relational Skills
1. Is he a good listener?
2. Can he share his faith skillfully?

KNOWLEDGE

Of the Word
1. Does he have a full understanding of the gospel?
2. Does he know his way around the Bible?

3. Does he understand and support your church's doctrinal statement?

Of the Church
1. Does he understand the ministry philosophy and strategies of your church?
2. Does he understand the nature of the small group and its goals?

Of the Community
1. Does he know the demographics of your area?
2. Does he have a feel for the issues facing your community?

Those questions are also valuable for a potential leadership candidate to use in evaluating his own strengths and weaknesses or for any leader to do an occasional check on his own life. Simply substitute "I" for "he" as you read through the questions. Although answering the questions mentally will be useful, you will find you get a far more stringent evaluation if you take time to answer the questions in writing.

TASKS OF LEADERSHIP
◆

The small group leader should develop his group members in three major areas: *evangelizing* unbelievers, *establishing* all members in the faith, and *equipping* all to serve the Lord.

Evangelizing

In order for all in the small group to take part in evangelizing unbelievers the group must provide vital witnessing experiences with non-Christians. First, teach your members that the purpose of their love for one another is to be a visible witness to unbelievers. Be sure to pray regularly for unbelievers in your small group prayer time, and encourage your members to get basic training in evangelism. Providing outreach to new residents through "Welcome Wagon" kinds of programs is a good area for evangelism, and long-time residents can be reached through social activities and mission programs. Finally, the small group should provide accountability for its members in this area of evangelizing.

Establishing

The second goal, that leaders of small groups help all members—old and newly evangelized—to become established, requires growing in two areas: in a community and in the faith. For most people relational experiences will precede religious experiences, so leaders should work first to assist members of their group to practice loving, serving, and building up one another. It is also important to assist your members to function well in their own roles as husband, wife, parent, single, older man, younger man, older woman, younger woman. Each member of the group needs to identify his or her own role and see the importance of it in relationship to the functioning of the whole body. In order for the community to remain vital, you need to integrate new people into the small group, because helping new people become established in the community is one of the best ways to help older members deepen their roots.

All leaders must lead their members deeper into the faith. They should help members grow in their knowledge of the Word, develop and maintain an active prayer ministry, grow in obedience to the Word, and deepen their worship of God.

As the family is the basic building block of society, so the church is the basic building block of the kingdom of God. Therefore, all members must be equipped to serve the body —in the small group, in the church, and in the community. Once we are established in our own roles, we must then be equipped to serve: "For the equipping of the saints for the work of service, to the building up of the body of Christ" (Eph. 4:12).

Equipping

Although all will serve the body in some capacity, there is a special call for some to lead. As 2 Timothy 2:2 exhorts, "And the things which you have heard from me in the presence of many witnesses, these entrust to faithful men, who will be able to teach others also." It is a special task of the small group leader to identify those faithful men who are to be teachers and to train them for leadership. The leader can do that in several ways. First, develop a special relationship with potential leaders—meeting personally with them in groups of two or three on a regular basis. Second, give them increasing ministry responsibilities in the small group. Third, by providing interaction and accountability, encourage them to develop character and the qualities of an elder. And finally, build up potential leaders in their knowledge by encouraging them to ever deeper Bible study.

When David Flavell first encountered that explanation of the major responsibilities of the small group leader, it was almost enough to make him back out of the whole thing. It is, indeed, an awesome list, and many of your leaders may feel equally overwhelmed. Examine the following list of goals, and encourage your leaders to take this one step at a time. The entire list of responsibilities for evangelizing are daunting, but any leader should be able take a few minutes in a small group meeting to share his own involvement in the life of an unbeliever. What has he done to model Christ to his neighbors? How has he set a Christian example in the workplace? What opportunities has he had to share his faith overtly? Once step one has been taken, it will not be difficult to go on to the second: to teach evangelism in the small group—perhaps by role-playing how to share your faith.

By the time David had read carefully through the following examples and imagined himself doing most of them, he had regained his confidence. No one could do all these at once—nor should he; it would be far too much for the group to assimilate. But over a period of time, perhaps working on one to three steps per meeting, they will all become a natural part of your small group ministry.

GOALS FOR SMALL GROUP PASTORS
◆

EVANGELIZING

1. To model active relational outreach
   Example: Share your own involvement in the lives of unbelievers.
2. To teach on evangelism regularly
   Example: Role-play how to share your faith.
3. To assist parents in sharing their faith with their children
   Example: Plan family events oriented toward the children.
4. To create an open, accepting environment
   Example: Have meetings that will be nonthreatening for unbelieving spouses.
5. To pray regularly for unbelievers
   Example: Have members keep a prayer list.
6. To visit and follow up on church visitors
   Example: Host visitors at Sunday services, and invite them to your small group.
7. To provide small group outreach events for unbelievers
   Example: Plan Labor Day picnic, Christmas party.
8. To provide accountability for members in evangelizing
   Example: Encourage members to get together with an unbeliever once a month.

9. To provide regular opportunities for members to share their experiences in evangelism
Example: Provide testimonials and encouraging experiences.
10. To provide opportunities for members to participate in missions
Example: Adopt a missionary family.

ESTABLISHING

In a Community
1. To know your people
Example: Call them during the week; listen to their needs.
2. To create an environment and opportunities for genuine personal sharing
Example: Model genuine personal sharing.
3. To assist husbands, wives, parents, and so on in their roles
Example: Plan men's and women's meetings to discuss roles.
4. To help members understand and practice the "one anothers"
Example: Encourage relationships with one another outside small group meetings.
5. To model spiritual maturity, especially older men/women to younger men/women
Example: Have older couples "adopt" younger couples; couples adopt a single adult.
6. To integrate new people into the life of the small group
Example: Invite new people over for dinner.

In the Faith
To assist members to:
1. Become established in the essentials of the faith
Example: Encourage them to work through a study series.

2. Grow in the Word
   Example: Lead interactive Bible discussions.
3. Maintain sound doctrine
   Example: Be alert to false teaching.
4. Grow in obedience to the Word
   Example: Provide one-to-one accountability.
5. Take corporate teaching into life
   Example: Discuss application of Sunday morning's message.
6. Develop and maintain an active prayer life
   Example: Keep a small group prayer journal.
7. Deepen and practice the worship of God
   Example: Celebrate the Lord's Supper.

EQUIPPING

All to Serve
1. To model service as a leader
   Example: Teach in the Sunday school; serve on hospitality team.
2. To affirm that every person is an important member of the body
   Example: Teach on 1 Corinthians 12 and Ephesians 4.
3. To delegate responsibilities to other members
   Example: Select or appoint people to duties.
4. To encourage *everyone* to be involved in the small group, the church, and the community
   Example: Publicly recognize people who serve.
5. To provide opportunities for the small group to serve as a whole group
   Example: Work at the community center.

Some to Lead
1. To select potential leaders
   Example: Pray for and be alert to potential leaders in the small group.

2. To develop relationships with potential leaders
   Example: Meet personally with 1-3 people on a regular basis for modeling and interaction.
3. To provide interaction and accountability for character growth
   Example: Work through *Measure of a Man/Woman*.
4. To assist potential leaders to have strong, solid marriages and families
   Example: Meet together as families.
5. To help them develop leadership skills by delegating responsibilities with supervision
   Example: Give them responsibility over a cell group within the small group.
6. To encourage potential leaders to get formal training
   Example: Take a course yourself and invite potential leaders.

STYLES OF INFLUENCE
♦

At the first leadership training meeting Gene Getz recommends having each potential leader take a Style of Influence (SOI) Questionnaire. (For more information see Appendix A.) When the trainee has completed the questions and scoring, he spends time thinking about his answers to the sentence completions: How do you think? How do you relate to others? How task-oriented are you? How much of a detail person are you? Then he has a conference with the staff member in charge of leadership training. The potential leader is counseled on how to be more effective in each area of thinking, relating, goal achievement, and detail management. Then he is helped to identify his greatest strength. Finally, he sets a goal for the area where he would most like to grow.

When preparing for leadership in a small group, self-understanding is of vital importance. The leader begins to understand why he does things the way he does and how to avoid actions that decrease his effectiveness. It is also important to identify his areas of weakness so that he can choose an assistant who is strong in his weak areas. A strongly cognitive leader will probably need an assistant who is more relational. A leader who is weak in dealing with details will need an assistant to handle the detail work. The better the leader understands himself, the more effective his leadership can be.

COMMITMENT AND ACCOUNTABILITY

Developing a high commitment level in your leaders is essential for developing commitment in your membership. Once they have made the initial commitment, leaders should agree to do the following:

1. Attend the prayer meetings of a small group consisting of small group leaders who are themselves under the leadership of a lay elder and a staff pastor, with their wives.
2. Attend leadership meetings as announced.
3. Attend various leadership functions, such as retreats, workshops, and training sessions.
4. Be a faithful steward financially by supporting the ministry of your local church on a regular and systematic basis.

Such commitments should not be viewed legalistically, and there certainly may be exceptions. However, leadership people should make every effort to maintain them.

You might want to use the following job description as a pattern.

SMALL GROUP LEADER JOB DESCRIPTION[3]

——◆——

I. Personal Ministry

Objective—To maintain a strong personal walk with the Lord by continuing in the spiritual disciplines that are necessary for "spiritual fitness" and growth in the grace and knowledge of God

Goals

A. Spend time in the Bible each day, pursuing personal growth and maturity.

B. Have a consistent prayer life that focuses on praise, thanksgiving, personal needs, the needs of believers, and the needs of the lost.

C. Spend time in spiritual fellowship with others for the purposes of mutual love, encouragement, and growth.

D. Be involved in fulfilling the Great Commission by reaching out to the lost, both in word and deed.

II. Small Group Ministry

Objective—To lead and disciple a small group of believers toward spiritual maturity in Christ

Goals

A. Plan a schedule of small group meetings for approximately six months at a time.

B. Have small group meetings at least twice a month.

C. Be responsible for making sure that each small group member knows where and when each meeting takes place.

D. Develop a format for the small group that embraces the three vital experiences necessary for spiritual growth.

  1. Dynamic learning experiences with the Word of God (Bible study)

2. Vital relational experiences with one another and with God (worship, sharing, prayer, breaking of bread, "one another" concepts, and so on)
3. Vital witnessing experiences with non-Christians (evangelistic "parties," personal evangelism, community outreach, mission emphasis, and so on)

E. Plan for social times (children included) that will promote *everlasting* friendships (picnics, pool parties, dinners).
F. Be available to teach, admonish, and counsel one-on-one with group members when the need arises.
G. Be available to advise or help meet the physical and material needs of group members when the need arises.
H. Maintain personal communication and contact with each group member.
I. Pray regularly for the needs of the small group both personally and corporately with other leaders.
J. Be committed to attend the care pastor meetings once a month.
K. Be accountable to your care pastor for your small group ministry.
L. Attempt to develop and disciple potential leadership within the group to help fulfill future growth needs of the church.
M. Delegate small group responsibilities to your support leader and other committed people in the small group.

One of the most important aspects of the small group is that it develops accountability. Members are accountable to other members and to their leaders. Leaders are accountable to their care pastors and to the staff, care pastors are accountable to the senior pastor. In one church each staff member has an accountability partner with whom he discusses questions and draws prayer requests from the discussion. "I need to spend more time studying the Word. Pray for me this week." "I need to be a better witness. Please pray for me." "I watched a television program this week that didn't glorify God, and it has left a residue of stain in my mind. Please pray for me." Each step of the way, everyone involved in the small group program is accountable to another person, just as they are accountable spiritually to God.

Small group leaders are likewise encouraged to pair up with their support leader for accountability. Finally, they often pair up the men in the small group to meet for sharing needs and prayer during the week. Women need to be accountable too, of course, but often women do this more readily on their own. By contrast, men need to be programmed and given guidelines, or they'll never open up to each other.

An accountability check can be used to help make the role of the leader clear. It can also be used as a guideline for one-on-one accountability among staff pastors.

ACCOUNTABILITY

1. How often did you meet with God this week?
2. What has God been saying to you through His Word this week?
3. What sins in your personal or business life did you commit this week that you need to confess?
4. How did you impact your marriage and family this week? Positively? Negatively? What could you do to improve?
5. Did you pray for me/us this week?
6. What challenges or struggles are weighing on your mind?
7. What lives did you impact for Christ this week?
8. Are you giving to the Lord's work regularly and proportionately as God has blessed you? What percentage did you give last month?

9. What movies did you see this past week? Would you be willing to tell the whole congregation what you've seen?

At this point, most of your selected leaders will probably be feeling about the way Susan Flavell did when she turned to her husband with an alarmed look in her eyes and asked, "What have we got ourselves into?" Perhaps just three stories of shaky starts by leaders who went on to lead successful small groups will be comforting.

Kenneth recalls, "I'll never forget the night I stood with five others in front of a room full of new small group members to be introduced as their leaders. I stood there trying to smile confidently, but the smile and the confidence evaporated when a man boomed out from the back row, 'What qualifies them to be our leaders?' That was exactly what I was asking myself.

"'They've had training,' our pastor said. 'These men are pastors—lay pastors.' Remembering that I *was* trained and realizing our pastor had faith in me made my knees quit knocking."

Kevin says he became a small group leader with great reluctance because he thought everyone else in the church had a strong Bible background and strong marriages. "At first I wondered how I could lead people like that. Then I decided, *Oh well, they've got it all together, so they'll be easy to lead.*

"I soon discovered the truth—they knew far less Scripture than I did, and they expected me to teach them. Next a couple in our group who had been married for twenty years got a divorce. I really felt inadequate then.

"But I got good support from my care pastor group, so I hung on. We've been leading a group for ten years now. I still don't know as much Scripture as I'd like to, but it's been a great experience."

Tanner smiles sheepishly before telling his story. "I was always nervous before I had to lead a group. I worked really hard to be prepared and to do a good job. Then one night during sharing time one of our members said, 'Tanner, you're a good leader, but you're not a comedian. You are not funny. Just relax and be yourself.'

"That was such a release! I didn't have to tell jokes! I did relax and started enjoying leading a small group in my style, not someone else's."

CHAPTER FIVE

◆

Laying the Groundwork 2: Logistics

*I*t was during morning coffee break on the second day of Bethany Bible Church's meetings about small groups that Betty Jo approached Susan Flavell. Barely more than five feet, Betty Jo always walked with a spring in her step that kept her mop of black curls bouncing, but today nothing about her bounced. "Susan, can I talk to you? Privately?"

Carrying her coffee, Susan led the way to the empty nursery across from the Fellowship Hall, and both women sank into rocking chairs. "What is it, Betty Jo? I've never seen you look so worried."

"What am I going to do, Susan? I've never felt like such a hypocrite in my life. All day yesterday I sat there and nodded and smiled, and whenever anybody said, 'Doesn't this sound great!' I'd nod and smile some more because my husband is chairman of the board of elders and I'm the last person who should be a wet blanket."

Susan set her half-empty cup down. She had her own concerns about the program, but Betty Jo's sounded much more serious. "Tell me—what's the matter? Doesn't James agree with all this?"

"Oh, yes—that's part of my problem—James is as excited as everyone else. You know we've only been married five years—before that I lived in Michigan until my first husband died. Maybe that's one reason I don't want to go into all this with James—neither of us talks much about our deceased spouses—but that's not the point. My problem is that I've had some really bad experiences with this small group thing. So, in the first place, I can't be all excited like everyone else, and in the second place, what if it goes badly here? If I don't say anything, I'll be responsible."

"What were your bad experiences?"

"Well, our church in Michigan tried three different small group programs in the seven years we were there. First was something they called care groups that I never did figure out, because no one understood it. We were so confused we never even went to a meeting. I guess that just died. Then a couple of years later our pastor read a book about something called prayer cells, and so the whole church was divided into these cells, and we got together in people's homes once a week to pray. Maybe we went once or twice—but it was so *cold*—emotionally, I mean—never mind the snow outside—I couldn't stand to go back.

"And then they tried home Bible studies—oh, that was the fourth—there were discipling groups in there somewhere, too, where we all tried to memorize a lot of Scripture. At least

I can still remember some of the verses—that was *something* good. But then the Bible studies—I think they were still hanging on when I moved. They were really boring, but there was this terrible guilt trip if you didn't go, so we went—but I just *can't* go back into something like that again, and I don't want that to happen to Bethany Bible, because it was discouraging —embarrassing really—for the whole church."

Susan gave her chair a gentle rock. She'd been listening so intently to Betty Jo that she had sat stock still through the whole narrative. "Good grief, you have been through the wars. I'd call you a burnout victim, except that usually means you worked so hard you got exhausted, and this sounds like none of your programs got off the ground well enough for anyone to work themselves into a burnout."

Betty Jo nodded, and this time her curls did bounce a bit. Just talking about the problem was a relief. "Oh, I forgot— there were evangelism outreach small groups, too. But never mind that. What am I going to do about my own negative feelings, and how can we keep something like that from happening here?"

Susan considered for the space of three back-and-forth rocks. "Well, now that you've taken the plunge and told me about it, how about going one step further and asking Eric Lions? After all, that's why the board brought an expert in. Surely he's run into situations like this before."

Betty Jo agreed, and the women cornered Eric in the Fellowship Hall just before the meeting resumed in the sanctuary. He listened quietly to Betty's recital, nodding with understanding. "You have no idea how often we hear similar stories—although I do think your experience of five attempts in seven years must be something of a record. You've got to give that church high marks for stamina—someone there cares enough to try." Then his expression became more serious. "But really, that's the heartbreaking part of a story like that. None of that needed to happen if the proper groundwork had been done first. It sounds like every time the pastor read a good book, he just announced a 'new program.' The way your church here is approaching this, with what will be weeks or even months of planning, training, and organization, should ensure against the kind of failure you described."

"Yes, I hope so." Betty Jo sounded hopeful but not convinced.

"As to your own feelings, I think there's only one way you can really catch a vision that will erase the negative pictures in your mind, and that's to visit a good small group in action. No amount of films or books will really give you the experience. I tell people small groups have to be caught, not taught."

"Sounds good, but where do I go?"

Eric considered for a minute. "Well, I'm not sure what's available within an easy drive from here. But we could find out. Serendipity and Navigators both maintain lists of churches with active small group programs,[1] or Pastor Tudway could ask at the next pastors' fellowship meeting what churches are doing around here."

As they walked toward the sanctuary together, Betty Jo's bounce was back. "Thank you both so much. Just talking really helped me—I don't feel like such a hypocrite now. And it helps to know that my experience isn't all that unique."

Because we have heard unfortunate stories like Betty Jo's again and again, we urge anyone starting a small group program for the first time or trying to revitalize a gasping program like the one Betty Jo left behind to pay special attention to the groundwork details outlined in this and the previous chapter.

WHAT'S YOUR STYLE?

◆

The next decisions you will have to make are about logistics. What will best suit the needs of your people and your church? There are as many styles of small groups operating in churches today as there are needs of people. The varieties include growth groups, Bible studies, discipleship groups, mothers' support groups, dinner clubs, book discussion groups, family life groups, care groups, and so on. Their names indicate their focus and the kinds of needs they focus on.

Specifically, the small group attempts to meet the following objectives.

1. Equipping believers for the work of the ministry (Eph. 4:12)
2. Developing and expressing faith, hope, and love within the body (1 Cor. 13:13)
3. Meeting biblical responsibilities toward other members of the body (Gal. 6:2, 1 Thess. 4:18, Heb. 10:24, James 5:16, 1 Pet. 4:9)
4. Communicating the gospel to a neighborhood through coordinated efforts (2 Cor. 5:18-19)

No matter what style group you choose, it is essential that your group be a "process group." There are two kinds of groups—educational groups and process groups. Educational groups teach what the Bible says; they teach facts. That's easier, but if it's all you do, you're only doing half the job.

Process groups help members apply knowledge to their lives. In the Minirth-Meier hospitals, patients are in small groups for two and a half hours a day, seven days a week. We spend one hour a day on education—looking at what the Bible says about anxiety, for example. Then we spend one and a half hours in process—sharing pains, learning together, comforting each other, and speaking the truth in love. That's what small groups must do. We are not advocating, of course, that small groups in the church function as "therapy groups"; what we are saying is that all effective small groups will share certain dynamics.

It's important that a group be a *growth* group, as opposed to a task group or a strictly fellowship group. Tasks such as Bible study and outreach programs are important, as is fellowship, but the spiritual growth of members has to be the primary focus of the group.

WHICH STRUCTURES SERVE BEST?
◆

Just as the names of small groups are nearly limitless, so are the varieties of structure. We would like to discuss just three elements of small group structure: leadership, membership, and size.

Leadership

From the foregoing discussion of choosing and training leaders, you have seen that we believe in the importance of strong leaders in a successful small group program. Some groups, however, have found leaderless groups to work well in certain circumstances.

Paul Meier's small group became semi-leaderless when he became burned out, so the coleaders took turns being in charge of meetings. In a leaderless group there is more emphasis on fellowship and socialization. Such groups aren't very demanding as there is less teaching and counseling.

A leaderless group can work well when all members are strong Christians. But even then, natural leaders will emerge. For example, the host and hostess of the home you are meeting in will naturally be in leading positions.

The greatest danger is that leaderless groups may become selfish because they lack focus. Such groups usually die after a period of time. A strong, ongoing program needs strong, committed leaders.

Membership

Another point to discuss is whether the group is open (new members can join at any time) or closed (no new members can be added for a designated period of time). Usually a new group should remain closed to new members for a period of time until strong bonding has developed between the core members. A closed group provides great security and promotes open sharing.

In addition, it may be helpful for a group to be closed for a specified period of time to accomplish a certain goal— such as an in-depth study that requires special materials and a high commitment level.

A group that stays closed permanently, however, can become stagnant and ingrown. It will feed on its own problems. And a small group that permanently closes its doors to new members cannot fulfill its role of evangelism.

Size

The third element of structure is size. The authors of this book, however, do not agree on the ideal size for a small group. Paul Meier and Allen Doran have had the most successful experience in groups that number between eight and fifteen, with twelve seeming to be the optimum. Twelve members is a small enough group for intimate bonding and yet allows for enough differences to avoid stagnation. It's also a comfortable number for most homes to handle. Although Dr. Doran doesn't claim that Christ was laying down a biblical principle when He chose His disciples, he points out that twelve was the number He chose for His small group.

Gene Getz, however, says his small groups function best with twelve to fifteen couples—at least twice the number many consider optimum. He suggests with a grin that maybe it's just that they like things big in Texas. But in order to mirror the church, with all levels of maturity—including singles and non-Christian spouses—the small group may need to be a little larger. The larger size also guarantees more anonymity, something some people need until they develop a sense of security in the group.

ARE THE NITTY-GRITTIES ORGANIZED?
◆

The what, when, and where details need to be organized before the small group ministry is presented to the congregation as a whole, because the smooth running of mechanical details will give members a sense of security and indicate that this is a worthwhile commitment for them to make. The first challenge for most churches is how to fit the small group structure into already existing programs.

When?

Gene Getz says it was easy for him to fit small groups into the schedule because he started the Fellowship Bible Churches with small groups as part of the original concept. Establishing them from the ground up is, of course, the easiest way.

One should never attempt to superimpose the small group structure on a traditional structure. The key is to examine your existing programs. What's working? What isn't? Don't change structures that are working. But when you find a program that is not extremely effective, see how the small group could fit into that structure.

People vote on the success of a new approach to ministry by their attendance or absence. Many churches have less than 50 percent attendance at their Sunday evening services. Could you substitute small group meetings one or two Sunday nights a month? It's not unusual for Wednesday evening prayer meeting attendance to be less than 10 percent of the Sunday morning attendance in many churches. Could your church be ministering more effectively with small groups on Wednesday evenings?

How effective are your adult Sunday school classes? Sunday mornings are often too limited a time slot for an effective small group, but perhaps you could begin by having your adult Sunday school classes—or at least some of them—incorporate small groups into their structure. Do you have a home Bible study program that is losing its original luster—or never really took hold as you had hoped? Could that be expanded and revitalized as small groups? Sometimes large churches choose to parent a new church in their area and structure it from the beginning with small groups, often eliminating the traditional Sunday night service and midweek prayer meeting. Parents are encouraged to stay home with their families, instead, on those nights while accomplishing the purposes of those former traditional meetings in small group meetings twice a month.

However you choose to incorporate small groups into your structure, remember that the key is renewal for ministry. The purpose of the small group movement is not merely to revive longtime church members for their edification but to enliven the church so that it can reach out and fulfill the Great Commission. You will always want to keep in mind the overall structure of your body ministry and keep edification, fellowship, and evangelism in balance.

Where?

Once you decide when to meet and how often, the next decision is where to meet. Although some groups might find it convenient to meet at the church, especially if they are meeting while children and teens have other programs there, the overwhelming preference seems to be to meet in homes. This is a comfortable, workable pattern and is illustrated in Scripture. In Acts 2:46 we read that they went "from house to house." Those weren't necessarily *small* groups, however, for some of the houses in Bible times were large enough to accommodate congregations of five hundred. Yet in the first two centuries the church had no choice but to meet in homes.

Depending on what the group finds comfortable and convenient, they may want to meet in the same home every time —such as the leader's home or the home of the support couple—or they may want to pass the hosting function around. Hospitality is an important ministry, and we need to be sensitive to the Spirit's leading in what could seem to be routine matters.

Who?

Deciding when and where to meet, however, is much easier than deciding how to divide your congregation into groups. Groups can be formed on the basis of age, geography, age of children, interests—and the list goes on. You will want to make your own decision, but geography may be the best basis of division for your groups. Commitment can be linked to geography. Studies have shown that the farther you have to travel, the less likely you are to go somewhere.

It is best if you can keep your groups within local neighborhoods. This facilitates interaction—when someone is sick, you can take food before it gets cold; when there's an emergency, you can be there in a matter of minutes.

Richard Meier, however, says that age grouping seems to have worked best in his church, where they have eight couples to a group, all between the ages of forty to fifty. They have common doctrinal beliefs but are all at different stages of maturity, different economic and vocational backgrounds, and different political views. That variety makes for great groups, because they have a foundation of similarities and enough differences to be interesting.

Interest grouping is another method that can be effective. However, this requires more staff work. For example, prospective members may fill out questionnaires and discuss their interests with the staff person assigned to designate the groups. Interest grouping is probably most effective where there is a variety of study options. Allen Doran recalls a successful growth group that focused on reading and discussing books. If your church ministers to a college or university community, you might want to give this emphasis special consideration.

Dividing up on the basis of children's ages can be especially effective when the small groups have a lot of social times that include the whole family. However, age variety is important because generational learning comes from associating with people older and younger than ourselves, especially as the small group takes on the role of an extended family. The younger can learn from the older, and the elderly will feel needed. Variety is important, and we learn from our differences. Generations are as important in a church family as they are in a biological family. The three generations of grandfather, father, and son have been referred to as the "trinity" of the home. It is important to keep that in mind when we think of the small group as fulfilling the role of an extended family.

When considering the ages of children, baby-sitting is an important factor. Young couples will not be able to commit to a program unless their children are cared for. Allen Doran, who has a school-aged son and daughter, says that his favorite solution to this is to have the small group meet in his own home. That way his children can play in their rooms and go on to bed. If you have several couples with children in your small group, you could take turns meeting in their homes so they wouldn't have to get baby-sitters every time you meet.

Dr. Doran's second choice is to have a baby-sitter at the house where the small group is meeting and to take his children with him. That keeps the family together, and the kids feel part of the small group. They also get to know the other children in the group.

His last resort is to get a baby-sitter at home because it makes the kids feel left out of something they know is important to their parents. He doesn't like giving his children the message that "this is one of the most important things in my life, but you can't have a part in it."

Regardless of how you divide into groups, it's best to let people come together on a voluntary basis once the groups are established. People like choices. Their commitment is likely to be higher to something they choose themselves.

Establishing the mechanics of the small group program is important, but we must remember that small groups are living organisms. Each small group will develop its own distinctive personality and pattern of activities. That is the only way it can truly minister to the needs of its various members. There must always be room for change and growth, but the basic decisions of who, when, and where must be made before the program is launched, or you will have mass confusion.

RELATING TO OTHER MINISTRIES
◆

The small group, important as it is, should be only one part of the ministry of your church. Although the small group meets many needs, it does not necessarily meet every need a believer may have. Other ministries reach different individuals and provide opportunities to serve the body. For some people these ministries may constitute an alternative to small group membership. For example, singles often choose involvement in the singles ministry rather than a small group. Or they may choose to do both.

The small group must see itself as part of the total ministry of the church. One way to aid this perspective is to have the senior pastor or another staff member regularly visit the small groups as a reminder that the group is a facet of the larger church.

And everyone who is in a small group must be encouraged to take part in other ministries of the church. Other ministry opportunities include: working in children's Sunday school, working with teens, singles, hospitality, or music, helping with codependency or other recovery groups, Bible studies, and women's ministries. Everyone needs to have a part in the functioning of the whole body.

CHAPTER SIX

Going Public

*R*eady for the big day?" David Flavell kissed Susan's neck as he fastened the top button on the back of her soft peach dress.

Susan smiled wryly. "Well, as ready as I'll ever be, I guess. I'm convinced that this small group program is just what our church needs—and what I need, too. But standing up in front of the whole congregation as the wife of a leader —as if I had some great truths to impart—I don't know . . . "

"Jared, Debbie, time to go!" David called, and picked up his Bible. "Not just the *wife* of a leader—as a leader. We're a team. Just remember, we weren't chosen for having advanced college degrees or perfect lifestyles but for our desire to serve."

Later, when Susan was sitting on the platform with the six other husband-wife teams, including Betty Jo and James, she remembered David's words. Yes, that was the key—serving the Lord by serving others—and she'd never seen a method that appeared to be so perfectly designed for really serving as the opportunities the small group would present.

The congregation was well-prepared for this morning. Pastor Tudway had just completed a six-week series on the functions and activities of the early church, much of it based on Acts 2. But Susan's favorite sermon had been on Acts 5:42: "And daily in the temple, and in every house, they ceased not to teach and preach Jesus Christ" (KJV*). That seemed to her to be the clearest biblical model for them to develop in their own church—large group worship and small group fellowship.

And their Sunday school class, as well as two of the other adult classes, had been studying Gene Getz's One Another books. A sense of urgency seemed to be rising in their midst to do a better job of ministering to each other and reaching out to their community.

Now excitement was in the air. For the past three weeks there had been posters up at church, announcements from the pulpit, and articles in the midweek letter. Every effort had been made to communicate to every member of Bethany Bible that something exciting was taking place—something they wouldn't want to miss out on. And the congregation had responded. Nearly every seat in the sanctuary was filled.

Pastor Tudway was giving a strong message on the true meaning of *koinonia* as a horizontal and vertical experience: "And so we can see as we look at the book of Acts that the

---

* King James Version.

first-century Christians lived out their faith in *koinonia*—in true fellowship with one another and with God. As they ate together," he swept his arm in a horizontal gesture that included all those in the sanctuary, "they remembered the Lord." His arm swept upward demonstrating the vertical relationship.

"And as they prayed for one another," again the horizontal motion, "they were talking to God." And all heads turned upward following Pastor Tudway's vertical motion.

"As they shared their material possessions with one another, they were doing it for the Lord. And finally, as they taught one another with psalms, hymns, and spiritual songs, they were making melody in their hearts to the Lord." Again, the horizontal and vertical motions.

"Their relationships with one another and with God were so intricately interrelated that they could not be separated. Problems arise when Christians try to relate to God in a vacuum. And many people can't relate to each other in depth because they have no relationship with God. If we're going to grow spiritually and produce a mature church, we need continual exposure to the Word of God and dynamic relational experiences with one another and with God.

"Your church board and a group of leaders have just completed an intensive study of how we can better work out this approach in our church." Susan caught her breath as the pastor turned briefly to them. "Behind me are six couples who are going to explain this program to you and give you an opportunity to be part of this exciting experience."

Pastor Tudway sat down. George Carson and his wife, Nan, were the first to speak. They told of visiting George's sister's church and attending the small group she and her husband led. George's enthusiasm was evident as he recounted the love and acceptance he had seen in that group as they ate homemade chicken and noodles on mashed potatoes together, shared some of the highs and lows in their lives, and prayed for one another.

James told about the sessions the church leaders had had with Eric Lions. Then Betty Jo, with all her bounce back, shared her initial fears born of negative experiences. "After all that, when someone said 'small group' to me, I wanted to go hide under my bed. But then James and I visited a group in Meridian, and all I can say is you have to see it to believe it. Knowing what failure looks like, I recognized success when I saw it—and it's great!"

After Betty Jo, another couple talked about their sense of need for a small group experience and the training sessions they had completed for leadership.

Susan took a deep breath and sent up a quick prayer for help. They were next. David took several minutes explaining in his clear, orderly, businessman's way the logistics of how the program would work—meeting in small groups in people's homes on the first and third Sunday nights of each month and continuing with regular evening worship the other Sunday nights, as the church board had decided that that would be the easiest time to integrate small groups into the existing schedule of their church.

Then it was Susan's turn. Still praying, she moved closer to the microphone. "I'll bet a lot of you are just like me. I've been wanting a better way to reach out to people." As a purely instinctive gesture she extended her hands. Several heads nodded at her, and a woman in the third row even held her hand out in response. That was just the encouragement Susan needed. "I've been wanting to build closer relationships with many of you. But I've got my hands full already. My kids hate it when I say, 'There's only one of me,' but I feel that way so much of the time—there's not enough of me to go around. How am I going to make time for something else? First, let me say that I'm really pleased with the board's decision to have the small groups meet on Sunday nights—that won't take another night out of the week for us.

"But more important is the fact that I really believe this is one way God wants me to live out my Christian life—a great tool for developing those horizontal and vertical relationships Pastor Tudway just talked about. I hope you'll all pray about being involved in a small group and ask God where He wants you—and I look forward to the relationships I'll be building with some of you in our small group."

HELPING PEOPLE "OWN IT"
◆

It is important that the people in your church "own" their small group program. The leadership needs to come from the top down, but the desire for the program needs to come from the bottom up as well. In our illustration Pastor Tudway did a good job of that by laying the foundation scripturally through his series of sermons and the Sunday school studies. Eric Lions's visit and the biblical renewal videotapes inspired the church board, elders, and teachers, and gave them a good grasp of the principles behind the program. Then all that preparatory work culminated on the Sunday morning when the small group concept was presented to the congregation, and they were asked to sign up.

We can't overstress the importance of fully explaining the purpose and function of small groups before asking people to sign up. Confusion can be the greatest barrier to meaningful participation. Also, we have found that although Bible study is an important function of small groups, it is not the major item to stress when inviting people to join. People identify most quickly with the need for social interaction, a desire to share, and the need for the support of caring friends. They want to belong to a meaningful body of peers.

It's a good idea to communicate that small groups do perform an educational function, but the purpose is to grow from the study.

Involving lay leaders in the first public announcement will help your congregation identify this as "their" program, not something that's being pushed on them from the top.

In order to avoid leadership discouragement, it is important to understand that not everyone will choose to be in a small group. In the biggest church in the world, in Seoul, Korea, every person in Pastor Paul Cho's 500,000-member congregation participates in what they call "cell groups," but it is highly unusual to find such unanimity of action in a modern Western church. Probably the closest example in America is Willow Creek Community Church, located near Chicago, which is the second largest church in America. Their fourteen thousand members attend approximately 280 small groups.

Appeal to your congregation's priorities, then let them make the decision. This program, like any other, is not for all of your people all of the time. It may be that God has called some individuals to something else. Each person will make his or her own decision before God.

But everyone should be informed of the opportunity and encouraged to join. Remind your people that even if you don't need others, others may need you. The stronger you are, the more you should use that strength for others. And remember, Scripture says we all need each other for input, for correction, and for accountability. Those who say they don't need anyone may be avoiding the biblical injunction to grow.

In order to avoid early discouragement with the program, work to develop realistic expectations. Be up-front about the fact that there is no such thing as a perfect group. Group leaders are trained, but they will make mistakes, just as members will. Encourage people to allow their group time to get started. Bonding takes time, and you are unlikely to see miracles of growth until the group is bonded. But it will happen, and the first step is to sign up.

You may want to distribute a form, such as this one.

THE SMALL GROUP

1. Please check one.
   _____ I (we) want to be placed in a small group.
   _____ I (we) do not wish to be placed in a small group at this time.

2. Do you have a preference for a specific small group?
   _____ No, please place me (us) in any small group.
   _____ Yes, I (we) would like to be in the _____ small group. (Please name the leader.)

3. Would you like to be grouped together in the small group with anyone from this orientation? Please list the people from orientation you would like to be with in the small group.

   _____

   _____

4. Do you have any preferences in terms of geographical location?
   _____ No.
   _____ Yes. (Please list.) _____

5. Do you have any preferences in age grouping of adults or children?
   _____ No.
   _____ Yes. (Please list.) _____

   _____

What is your age group?

__ 20-24	__ 35-39	__ 50-54
__ 25-29	__ 40-44	__ 55-59
__ 30-34	__ 45-49	__ 60 and over

6. Our small groups meet on Saturday or Sunday nights. Please check the night of your choice.

_____ Saturday _____ Sunday _____ Either

7. Your comments: _____

_____

8. NAME: _____
   ADDRESS: _____
              (Street)   *(City)*   *(State)* *(Zip)*
   PHONES: _____
              (Home)   *(His work)*   *(Her work)*

When the forms have been filled out and collected, tell people they will be contacted within a few days and assigned to a small group near them. Once you've built enthusiasm for the program, don't let it drop. Hold your first small group meetings within a week.

DEVELOPING COMMITMENT
◆

The importance of commitment to the small group must be stressed from the very beginning in order to avoid sporadic attendance, which will kill bonding. Members must be urged to place their small group very high on their list of personal priorities. It needs to be considered a highlight of the week.

Membership in a small group means commitment to a biblical relationship of service and personal involvement with other small group members. The New Testament makes

clear that every member of the body has the important function of building up the other members of the body (1 Cor.
12:12-17). Such a commitment obviously involves time and a
decision by members to make the small group a personal
priority.

Understanding the value of commitment can help today's
hang-loose generation overcome their negative reactions to
taking on obligations.

We have found a variety of analogies used to describe the
commitment members make to their small group. Some would
compare it to the relationship of a student to his school, of a
citizen to his country, or of contracting parties in a business.
Allen Doran's church uses the term *covenant,* which is perhaps the strongest term of all, because it recalls the covenant
God made with His people in the Old Testament and the New
Covenant that Christ decreed in the New Testament.

Gene Getz finds that the analogy of "extended family"
best describes the kind of commitment and relationship they
desire for their small group members. For many people their
biological families are far away, and they actually see their
small group as their family. In this relationship there is sharing of problems, crises, finances, dreams, and hopes in the
context of a caring family. Some go on camping trips, retreats, or other kinds of vacations together as a family would,
as well as exercising and playing together.

The idea of a family commitment may frighten some people because of the permanence it implies. Yet this permanence is its strength. The permanence found in a family is a
permanence of caring even when family members go off to
college, get married, or move away to take a new job. So in
the small group can letters and prayers follow "family" members.

Allen Doran has participated in small groups on both
sides of the continent and has observed that in the West he
found people committing in terms of a specific study or time

period, such as eight or twelve weeks, whereas on the East Coast he found a greater sense of permanence, so groups in that part of the country may have an easier time in the matter of commitment. Even in the West, however, the group will bond and grow better if the commitment is for up to two years, rather than only a matter of weeks or months.

Most experienced small group leaders recommend asking for a commitment of at least two years, with the goal of extending for a longer time. Many people have found that new groups take as long as three years to bond, but once that occurs with the core group, it is much easier for newcomers to be open in the meetings because the chemistry is already there. In the meantime, the uncommitted will drop out.

One leader whose group had met for two years without significant bonding taking place said, "We were just a bunch of people meeting for Bible study and small talk. Then there was a crisis in our group. A man had a seizure at a meeting. That caused people to open up. From then on, people were committed."

In spite of the importance of commitment, however, you can't demand it. In the small group, commitment requires maturity. Some people in your group will be immature. It's your job to bring them to maturity. Have your leader model commitment and develop the commitment of your core members. Then reach out to those who aren't yet ready to make the step of commitment. Try to make them feel comfortable and secure in the group—and pray for them. Don't judge them. You should encourage all your members to commit their time, talent, and treasures to the work of God, but you can't force that kind of dedication. Ultimately, the Holy Spirit must work in every person's heart.

Verbal contracting can be effective. Have your group agree on what's reasonable. One's children and mate will be more important to him or her than the small group. That's reasonable and desirable. But your commitment must run deeper than a willingness to go to your small group as long as there's not a better party going on somewhere else.

Small group membership should mirror your accountability to your own spiritual commitment—it's a way to live out your beliefs.

Paul Meier is committed to his growth group for life. As members die or move away, new couples may join, but no one plans just to quit. He wants to see the other members' kids grow up, graduate, marry, start their own families, and he wants to share the stages of family life with them. He wants to experience the joys, aches, and pains of old age with people he can trust, sharing his struggles and emotions with them.

One couple that has led a successful small group for many years explained how they have developed commitment in their group. "We always meet at least every two weeks. That's important for developing intimacy and continuity. And there are two things we always do at every meeting: first, we always have a full meal together. There's no substitute for the bonding that can occur in the family atmosphere around a dinner table. Second, we always have what we call high/low sharing. We share something that we're feeling good about and an area where we're struggling. We have found that it's important to focus on feelings rather than on circumstances. This helps prevent members' feeling overwhelmed by the problems of the group.

"We make commitment an up-front understanding. We ask for a seventy-five percent attendance commitment. We take role at every meeting, keep records, and follow up on member attendance. When someone has several unexplained absences, we call and say, 'We've missed you.' If the absence was something beyond their control, we say, 'OK, come back when you can.'

"If the continued absence is due to slipping commitment, however, we put them on a permanent visitor's list. They still get our calendar, and they can come when they want to, but that way we can invite another couple to fill their spot. We like to keep a stable membership of twelve to fifteen couples. When a couple goes on the permanent visitor's list, we keep their name tags ready for them and call them when we have a special program, but they're not on our prayer chain. If they decide they want to become active again, they can if there's space; if not, they go on a waiting list.

"We don't mean to be harsh or judgmental with anyone, but this system has kept a high degree of commitment in our group for about fifteen years."

It will help your small group members make deep commitments if other church programs are not competing for their time. Gene Getz's church is so thoroughly committed to their small group program that they drew up the following guidelines to help clear their members' calendars and free them for making a commitment to their small groups.

1. Decrease highlighting of other adult groups. In bulletin and church newsletter decrease the amount of communication about non-small group ministries and activities.
2. Increase the highlighting of small groups. In all church communications, increase emphasis on small group activities. Include news, praises, requests, and ideas from specific small groups in newsletter.
3. Set up pilot model small groups. Have several small groups experiment with format changes to see if they help achieve our goals.
4. Deny almost any requests for new adult ministries.

At first these may seem shockingly strict, but for Fellowship Bible Church North a major key to the success of their small group program has been the concept of modeling—setting the right example for others to copy. If the church doesn't set an example of commitment to small groups in arranging its calendar, you can't expect individual members to do so.

When we asked Mike Cornwall, an elder and small group leader, about commitment to a small group, he told a story of a young couple in the first group he led. "Their example taught me the most important lesson of my life about commitment. This couple were both missions students at the seminary. They drove an old car held together by baling wire and prayer. They were so poor that when our group had a potluck dinner, they would forage in the woods for berries in order to have something special to bring.

"Well, our group decided to go on a retreat together. They chose Pine Cove Lodge, which is a really nice Christian retreat center. Too nice, I was afraid, because it would be expensive. I figured it would cost at least seventy-five dollars a couple.

"Excitement in the group was really high over this event, but the higher the excitement rose, the more I worried. I knew those kids couldn't afford that retreat, and I didn't know what to do about it—that was before we'd thought of offering scholarships for things like that.

"Finally I decided I had to approach them about it, so I called Mark. 'You know,' I hem-hawed around. 'I'm worried about this retreat business. It's going to be awful expensive. I'm afraid some of the people in the group won't be able to afford to go.'

"Mark thought for a moment. 'Well, how much would they need?' he asked. 'Judy and I've got a little saved up for Christmas. We could help.'"

That kind of commitment comes from true bonding that is the very heart of the small group. That was not just the commitment of Mark and Judy, nor of Mike as their leader; that level of dedication only grows from the commitment of the whole church, from the top leadership down. Far too many churches have had experiences like the ones Betty Jo described to Susan Flavell at the beginning of chapter 5—they've sampled a "program" that didn't work, abandoned it, then tried another version a couple of years later. Worse, many churches are limping along with less-than-successful programs, which they hesitate to abandon but don't know how to revive. It is our experience that by carefully laying the groundwork through selecting and training leadership, through smoothly run logistics and a properly planned, fully supported launch such as we have described, even churches that have undergone burnout or blahs can enjoy the excitement of the small group phenomenon.

CHAPTER SEVEN

—◆—

*Experiencing
the Small Group*

*S*usan closed her eyes as she sank into a comfortable arm-
chair in Tessa's spacious family room decorated with
modern American art. Would tonight be any different? The
spaghetti dinner had been great—the September evening dis-
playing absolutely golden weather, the food delicious, the
conversation light and flowing. But now, would the sharing
go any deeper? They had been meeting twice a month ever
since last February. And, although everyone seemed to enjoy
the meetings, the sharing was often nonexistent and never
rose above the shallow. Would the group ever truly bond?

Surely there were people here with hurts, problems, needs. Surely someone needed help and prayer for more than "Jimmy, who has a tough exam tomorrow."

Of course Susan was glad to pray for Jimmy's exam and Shana's basketball game and Mervyn's business trip, but what about the deeper needs she knew existed? What about Al's alcohol problem and their shaky marriage? What about Mitzi's struggles as a single parent? The Crofts' little Sean was almost six months old now, and Susan had been the first from their small group to visit Janice in the hospital and hold the baby. They seemed happy, but she wondered, *Do they truly feel part of the church yet?*

As soon as everyone was gathered in the circle around the family room, Jerry Minchel, their support leader, brought out a cassette tape. "I've been listening to this every morning as I drive to work for about two weeks now, and I get a new insight every time I hear it. Let me play just a couple of songs for you." He crossed the room and inserted the tape in the tape deck. It was *A Mighty Fortress*, produced by Steve Green, with songs composed from each phrase of Martin Luther's classic hymn. While the music played, Susan thought about what a wonderful fortress and refuge God was—how He never failed to help and provide, no matter how big the hole in the bottom of the barrel looked to her.

And now it wasn't just a hole in the bottom—there wasn't even a bottom anymore. They had found out just two days ago. The bankruptcy trustee had finally sold the Megacorp building, and David had gone to the distribution hearing. They knew the real estate market was depressed, they knew an unfinished building wouldn't bring a very good price, they knew that although Flavell Construction was a secured creditor they came behind the tax liens—but they had thought there would be *something*.

David hadn't had to say a word when he came home. She could tell with one glance. He looked ten years older—gray, lined, and stooped. She had thrown her arms around him and said, "It's all right. We'll make it." And to prove that she believed her own words she added hamburger to the lasagna sauce for dinner and made a batch of chocolate chip cookies.

But in spite of her faith, she couldn't help thinking that Christmas was coming. Debbie and Jared wouldn't expect big gifts, but she did want to get them something. And Uncle Clarence was coming if he felt well enough. And Debbie really needed a new dress. Of course Susan would sew it, but fabric itself was expensive.

She started as the tape shut off. It wasn't really that she'd been worrying; it was more as if God had been showing her her needs. *But,* she argued, *those are just material things —they aren't really important, not like having a child on drugs or a brother in jail. Besides, I can't share that—it's David's problem more than mine, and he would be too embarrassed to talk about money problems in front of all these men.*

Her arguments continued, yet she couldn't shake the feeling that she ought to say something. But David was across the room, and she couldn't speak out without his permission. After all, he was the leader—what would they all think if they knew their *leader* had financial problems?

"Susan, you look like you have something to tell us." She blinked at David's voice, not sure she'd really heard him.

She looked at him from across the room with the level, communicating gaze they had developed through eighteen years of marriage. "Do you want me to share, David?" she asked as if they were alone in the room.

"Yes." He nodded.

And so she told the whole thing—how even though everyone thought they were rich and successful, Megacorp's bankruptcy had left them all but bankrupt, and it was only because of David's determination not to take the easy way out that they hadn't just given up—that and God's never-fail-ing provision. "But I do get tired," she finished. "I don't mind doing without myself—I really don't—but I hate having to tell the kids, 'We can't afford it,' every time they need something."

As she talked Susan had alternated between looking at her hands folded in her lap and stealing peeks at David. Now she raised her head and looked around the room. She couldn't believe it—there wasn't a dry eye in the circle. Even some of the men—Leon and Mike and Bo—were blowing their noses.

The group was quiet, but it was a comfortable silence. Susan felt love and warmth as if others had reached out to touch her. The quiet held for close to two minutes, then Tessa, sitting with her legs curled under her in a big hurricane chair, her blonde hair pixie-like around her gamin face, looking like a blonde Liza Minelli, started talking in a voice so soft that it was hard at first to locate the source of the words or to understand them.

"I've been wanting to share in here for weeks, but I've never had the nerve. You see, I always think I'm the only one with problems. I mean, the rest of you—you all *look* perfect. Susan, I'd never have guessed you had any problems. But I guess if you do, others might too, so I'll tell you—

"I don't think any of you know that I've been in recovery in Al-Anon for eight years now. I've had a real problem having a personal relationship with God because of the terrible relationship I had with my domineering, legalistic, alcoholic father. I want you to know that being in this group has been really healing to me. I never felt part of the big church service because I thought, *I'm not as good a Christian as these people—they all have perfect marriages.* But you women here are such great role models—you're so loving, and you let me know it's OK if I don't know where to find a book in the Bible. You are all better Christians that I am, but you've let me know that's OK. It's been great these past eight months to be with a group that never put me on the spot, never embarrassed me, never made me feel 'less than.'

"I went to the big church every Sunday, and I was OK as long as I could be anonymous. It was a big step when I got up the courage to come to a small group—I just knew you'd call on me to quote a Bible verse. I'll never forget how I panicked when we broke up into small groups—*Now I'm going to get it,* I thought. But there wasn't any pressure at all." She stopped talking with a big sniff.

Janice Croft was the first one on her feet to walk across the room with her arms open. Tessa jumped to her feet to meet Janice halfway, and they stood in the middle of the floor with their arms around each other. Mitzi was only a few steps behind Janice. In a few minutes about half the small group stood in an embrace in the center of the room, and the others sat around the circle holding hands. David began the singing very softly: "We are one in the bonds of love, we have joined our spirit with the Spirit of God, we are one in the bonds of love . . . "

THE SMALL GROUP MEETING
◆

The Flavell group is a good example of what a newly formed small group can expect—a good social time for several months, then some crisis in the group bringing out the strength the group has been quietly building. Our fictional group is a particularly good example because the lead couple modeled the openness that led others to be open.

One small group member recounted an example in his group that shows how openness can be sparked by a seemingly simple thing. "We were studying *The Man in the Mirror* and discussing how we were perceived in the workplace, especially regarding dirty jokes. One of the men in our group said, 'I don't want there to be one John Smith at home and one in the workplace.'

"A new girl who had spent the entire evening sitting quietly in the corner suddenly started crying at John's words. 'I don't know why I'm crying.' She mopped at her tears. 'I never do this.'

"Our leader's wife leaned over and hugged her. 'Welcome to the small group,' she said."

Achieving openness and oneness is what the small group is all about, and we have found that there are four activities that facilitate that. We don't necessarily do all of them with the same emphasis every meeting, but over a period of several meetings we always include: eating, Bible study, sharing, and prayer.

These activities help the group reach several goals: to provide personal Christian fellowship; to provide growth and spiritual maturity; and to support one another emotionally and spiritually.

EATING

◆

Again and again as we have interviewed members of successful small groups we have been reminded of the importance of eating together. And certainly there are biblical examples aplenty: Jesus feeding the five thousand, Jesus taking the Last Supper with His disciples, Jesus cooking fish on the seashore after His resurrection, and as Acts 2:46 records, "[They], breaking bread from house to house, did eat their meat with gladness and singleness of heart" (KJV).

One small group leader says, "One of the worst things you can do is let people come to a small group meeting and *just sit*. The best way to keep this from happening is to *eat*. We've always found that a full meal is best. Somehow the fellowship never seems as strong when we just have snacks."

The more you feed people, the more they bond. Sometimes Allen Doran's group comes together as a family around one big table, and other times they serve buffet style so that people can pair off to sit and eat in small groups. Some important talking gets done at times like that, he says.

Food makes people comfortable emotionally as well as physically. It's very important that people be comfortable before you begin your Bible study.

Food serves several important social functions. People open up more when they're eating; it gives them something to do with their hands; it makes the occasion more important, more festive; it breaks the ice; it's something to which you can invite outsiders.

Although some people said their groups alternated between having full meals and snacks, most agreed that full meals were best. It's really hard not to laugh together when you're sharing calories, and laughter is an open door to emotional closeness.

A group of Christians eating together is always a special event because it looks back to Christ's Last Supper with His disciples, and it looks forward to the Marriage Supper of the Lamb.

STUDYING

◆

One group leader, Larry Clough, described a typical evening. "First thing when people walk in we offer them a cup of coffee or a soft drink, so they'll feel comfortable standing around and visiting until everyone is there. Then we begin with a meal—or sometimes just refreshments.

"Then we move to our formal Bible study. We usually open with prayer, then sing and praise God together, then focus on the lesson. We often break up into smaller groups for discussion and sharing, then come back together for prayer.

"We most often recommend the Serendipity materials for our Bible studies.[1] They offer a series of inductive Bible studies for small groups and another series of lifestyle studies on such topics as career, family, money, stress, and success. We even send people to the Serendipity seminars for training," Larry said. "But we don't prescribe any certain study course for our small groups. Each group needs to study what will best suit its needs—whether it's a topical Bible study, a book of the Bible, or a good Christian book based on biblical principles. Whatever the choice, though, it must focus on the Bible because that's the only thing that's totally reliable." Some groups prefer working through a devotional book, such as *Free to Forgive,* by Paul Meier and Frank Minirth.

Knowing the fears some pastors have of putting this much responsibility into lay hands, we asked Larry whether he'd ever had any problem with groups choosing unsuitable study materials or leaders teaching unsound doctrine. His clear blue eyes widened for a moment while he thought, then shook his head in wonder. "Never. Never in eight years. Isn't that amazing! I believe that's because we choose our leaders so carefully and train them so well," he concluded.

The Serendipity *Bible for Groups* is especially helpful. It includes the complete NIV text with thousands of discussion questions and ready-made study courses on topics, Bible stories, and books.

Besides the Serendipity Bible studies, there are also excellent series published by groups such as The Navigators available at your Christian supply store.

Resources

You might prefer to design a study for your own group's needs. The first step in preparing a Bible study is to assemble your study helps. You will want to have several versions of the Bible available and at least one good study Bible. The *NIV*

Study Bible and the *Ryrie Study Bible* are two of the best. Such study Bibles contain copious footnotes explaining the text of the Scriptures, as well as useful maps, charts, tables, a concordance, and much other useful information.

Besides Bibles, you will find other study helps useful, such as a concordance, Bible dictionary, Bible handbook, and commentaries. Each of these helps differs in its approach to the material.

A concordance is an alphabetical index of the words in the Bible and gives textual references to the verses where the words are found. *Strong's Complete Concordance* lists every word in the Bible, including *a* and *the.* Young's and Cruden's are also very good concordances. A concordance is invaluable for developing a Bible study around a specific theme and for locating Bible verses.

A Bible dictionary contains alphabetical listings of objects, events, and people in the Bible with information about them, something like a short-form encyclopedia, often including small pictures or maps of the subject. *The New Unger's Bible Dictionary* is one of the best.

Halley's is a good example of another study help—the Bible handbook. This compact wealth of information can be easily carried as a ready reference. It contains notes on all the Scriptures, an outline of Bible history, comments on living the Christian life, Bible chronologies, maps, weights and measures tables, and archaeological notes.

Bible commentaries are a systematic series of explanations or interpretations of the Bible, usually comstituting many volumes. Commentaries are written from the commentator's viewpoint and as such can be very enlightening to Bible study but should not replace the Scripture itself or the guidance of the Holy Spirit in your own reflection and study. Tyndale's, Clark's, and Barclay's commentaries are among the most popular. Paul and Richard Meier's favorite commentary is Dallas Seminary's *The Bible Knowledge Commentary* (edited by John P. Walvoord and Roy B. Zook). They have found it to be extremely accurate, objective, and to the point.

Processes

Once you have chosen the topic you wish to study and have assembled your materials, the next step is to arrange your Bible study. All group Bible studies follow three basic processes: Bible reading, explanation, and application.

1. BIBLE READING

What does the Scripture say? This is the simplest, most direct part of the study. Don't let it become the most boring. The key here is to use variety in your methods of reading. Some possibilities: having members read from different translations, responsive reading, singing the Scripture (works best for Psalms), or dramatizing the Scripture. Sometimes something as simple as having the reader stand, or the listeners kneel will help the group focus on the Bible reading.

2. EXPLANATION

What does the Scripture mean? At this point in the study you want to make clear to your group the meaning of what they have just read. Here your work with the commentaries, Bible dictionaries, and so on mentioned above will be helpful. You needn't present pat answers. If you find that the commentators disagree, present both viewpoints. Archaeological information and historical perspective can be helpful at this point, but don't bury your group in it. The goal is to get them to think, not put them to sleep.

3. APPLICATION

What does the Scripture say to me? This is the part of the study where the rubber meets the road. If group members don't apply the Scripture to their lives, no amount of technical or historical information will have been of value. Each member needs to ask himself or herself, "What difference does this make in my life?" "How can I put this scriptural principle to use?"

Sometimes group members can best be encouraged to make personal application of the Scripture through quiet reflection, perhaps while quiet music is played in the background. Other times you might want to encourage members to write down their responses in the form of journaling or by outlining a set of goals. Most often, however, people will make the best application through group discussion. Even the more solitary approaches mentioned above should be followed by opportunities for discussion.

Small group discussion will encourage sharing of opinions and feelings and discourage narrow-mindedness and isolation. It gives all an opportunity to discover new ideas and test their own. Discussion also demands active participation rather than passive listening and stimulates learning through the flow of ideas. Whatever techniques you choose to employ for a certain lesson, however, be sure that your Bible study has take-home value.

Fellowship Bible Church North distributes a Bible study outline to all of its members each week based on this three-part plan. These can be used for the small group or for individual study. The culmination of the week's study then is a sermon on that topic Sunday morning.

Here is a three-day's sample of this study.

BIBLE READING AND STUDY GUIDE

◆

This week we will study how to have stable lives and be fruitful despite crises or bad circumstances.

OCTOBER 7

Bible Reading: Psalm 1:1-3; Colossians 1:6, 9-12

Explanation: The Scripture says that the man who turns away from worldly, sinful philosophies and behavior and knows God's Word is a blessed (happy, joyful) man. Paul's prayer for the Colossians was that God would make His will known to them, which would enable them to live a worthy life. The goal for them was bearing fruit in every good work.

Application: God wants fruitful Christians. Many Christians are unhappy and barren. "As with a tree, more times than not the surface problem is only the symptom of a deeper issue. Their branches are dry and barren because there is something wrong with the root system and they are not feeding on the nourishment in the soil" (Neil Anderson). Spraying the leaves won't help the tree, nor will attempting to manipulate or change the outside conditions solve the problem of a barren Christian.

OCTOBER 8

Bible Reading: Psalm 1:1-3; Romans 12:1-2; Colossians 2:8-10

Explanation: The psalmist lays down a prescription for the man (or woman) of God to live a happy, fruitful life. The beginning is not to walk, stand, or sit in the ways (philosophy and lifestyle) of the ungodly, worldly sinners. It means that we don't copy them, think like them, talk like them, or live like them in any area of life. Paul says we are not to be conformed to the world, not pressured or squeezed into its mold and pattern. Philosophy and human traditions that are not biblically based are hollow, even deceptive. They may present their way to happiness, but in the end destruction will result.

Application: Christians who will not wholly commit to God's Word, but instead keep a foot in both worlds, will be unhappy, barren Christians. As Billy Graham said, if you are going the way everyone else is going, you had better stop and check your directions. Worldly philosophies may sound clever, even scholarly, but in the end they will destroy you. As a Christian, you almost have to go "counter-culture" and swim upstream, because the force of carnality and godlessness in our society is all-pervasive.

OCTOBER 9

Bible Reading: Psalm 1:1-3; Colossians 1:9-12; 2:1-7

Explanation: The psalmist's positive instruction is to meditate on God's Word. That means to know it and apply it to life's problems. Being able to stand on God's Word to order our philosophy of life, the principles we live by, and the values we hold will enable us to be fruitful in good times and during crisis. Like a tree root tapping into an underground water source, the Word of God gives spiritual nourishment to Christians. In Colossians 2, Paul uses the same word *rooted* as a metaphor for knowing Christ more completely.

Application: Neil Anderson says that many Christians are trying to act or live a maturing lifestyle without first being rooted in Christ. They don't know their identity in Christ. Their knowledge of the Word is incomplete and even superficial. Consequently, when the inevitable problems appear, they crumble or fall back on carnal solutions. They are like trees with puny roots. How is your root system? Are you feeding on God's Word?

Besides group study, members should be encouraged to develop their personal Bible study time at home. The following chart can be useful in getting members started on their own study. You will note that it, too, follows the three-step approach to group study.

PERSONAL BIBLE STUDY GUIDE

◆

PASSAGE: _____ TITLE: _____ DATE: _____

1. PRAY - Praise God and ask Him through the Holy Spirit to illuminate your mind.
2. SURVEY - Read the passage quickly.
3. READ - Read the passage carefully.
4. OBSERVE - Look for biblical statements that are especially meaningful. Copy these statements in column 1.

5. INTERPRET - Record in column 2 what those biblical statements mean. Note: Be sure to consider the larger context.
6. APPLY - Record in column 3 what you can do to apply these statements in your life.
7. PRAY - Use your observations and applications as a basis for prayer and praise.
8. SHARE - Look for a natural opportunity to encourage someone with what you have learned.

READING AND RECORDING

What does the Bible say? Copy key statements and verses from the passage.

_____

_____

_____

_____

INTERPRETING AND UNDERSTANDING

What do these statements mean? Put in your own words (outline, ask questions, and so on).

_____

_____

_____

_____

APPLYING AND OBEYING

How do these statements apply to my life?

What will I do? _____

When will I do it? _____

With whom will I do it? _____

Another example of three-part Bible study that has proved very successful in small groups is the Body Builder series that Gene Getz's church uses. Each lesson begins with a personal question to get the individual to think about his own background, and it provides ideas on a topic related to the passage. The Scripture reading is printed out, followed by questions pertaining to the Scripture. Application follows: What has God taught you about this subject? How can you show Christian concern better? What are you going to do about this? Then the lesson concludes with two short assignments for the following week, such as Scripture memory, prayer, or action. Samples of these lessons are included in Appendix B. You may want to design your own lessons following this format.

Expanded Topics

It is a good idea for new groups to start with a Bible study. That approach will serve as a bridge between those who are comfortable with the traditional Sunday school and those who are more open to the newer, small group approach. A Bible study with lots of personal application is best at first. Once the group has matured you can expand to cover a variety of interests.

Besides Bible studies, many groups find studies of Christian books extremely helpful. Books can be chosen to meet any need the group expresses. Marriage and parenting are usually at the top of the list. Christian psychology books are excellent for this purpose as long as they are doctrinally sound, use lots of Scripture, and are applicable. For example, a small group could work through Larry Crabb's *Inside Out*.

Studying contemporary issues can also be beneficial. Small groups can serve as a sounding board in discussion of issues that chink away at our Christian armor or things in society that attack our families.

Whatever approach you choose, it's important that leaders and group members have a voice in the decision. Paul Meier says he's been in small groups where the church staff designed the lesson to be used for each small group meeting, but he doesn't recommend that. He found that leaders and groups resisted that approach since they had not been given the freedom to adapt.

In Richard Meier's small group he prepares an outline of the lesson for each meeting and sends it to each member. All study in advance and come to the meeting prepared, which makes for good discussion. Each member is challenged to do his own research and to make applications to his own life or to ask for help in making applications.

He has also compiled a list of possible courses of study for his group. When they need to select a new topic he passes the sheet out and the group members mark what they want to study. His list of topics may help you come up with ideas for your group to study.

> Assurance of salvation
> Personal quiet times
> Inspiration of the Scripture
> Bible study methods
> How to give a testimony
> How to share the gospel with the lost
> How to have victory over entangling habits
> Developing priorities
> How to express Christian love
> Principles for knowing right from wrong
> Knowing the will of God
> Spiritual gifts
> How to meditate on the Word
> Basics of Bible prophecy
> Settling personal offenses

One church has a tape and video library for small groups. They can choose a series from such leaders as Chuck Swindoll, James Dobson, or Charles Colson. They run the tapes and follow them with discussion. It's a great way to get big-name guest speakers for your small group.

SHARING
◆

It is undoubtedly apparent that the most crucial aspect of a small group meeting for producing bonding and growth is the sharing time. And the key to successful bonding and sharing is the ability to trust others. Because trust can only be based on experience, it must be earned over a period of time. Therefore it may take years for fully open sharing such as we saw in the Flavell group to occur. You can do several things, however, to help speed up the process.

We have already mentioned the importance of focusing on highs as well as lows to keep the sharing from becoming overwhelmingly depressing. Jim and Becki Terral, coleaders with Richard and Lorraine Meier, said, "Another thing we've found to be important is not allowing too many details in prayer requests, especially if someone is requesting prayer for a situation outside his immediate family." If he needs to talk in more detail, that can be done later with the leader in private. "Problems in our immediate family, however, we share in detail," Jim said. "For example, one evening a woman shared in depth about some in-law problems she was having. Her honesty prompted good sharing for the whole evening—it seems as if one person's openness serves as a key to opening up feelings others have kept locked away."

Strange as it may seem, that kind of open sharing actually discourages rumors. Openness eliminates the "need" some people have to talk about other people's problems. In fact, it creates trust and loyalty and a commitment to protect one another.

It is also important to realize that not all sharing takes place during the formal sharing time. One woman said that a breakthrough came the evening a staff pastor and his wife came to their small group as special guests to lead a study on marriage. She was in awe of them because they were "beautiful people" and always seemed to have everything together.

"They arrived late," she recalls. "We'd begun to wonder what had happened. Finally the pastor's wife stomped in and stood in the middle of the room with her hands on her hips. 'All right,' she said. 'Everyone who had a fight on their way here tonight raise your hand.'

"Of course we about died laughing, but also several hands went up. Later, when the pastor and his wife taught a lesson on resolving marital conflict, we really listened, and no one was afraid to open up."

Another leader says it's important for the leader to lose control sometimes. People need the freedom to share honest emotions, and a leader should allow time for this. "It happens most often with humor in our group. But I find that if I give them the freedom to be really silly for a while, some deep sharing often follows later."

Richard Meier says he likes to start his groups on an upbeat. They start by sharing their personal blessings and try to spend at least fifteen minutes on praises. Then they move on to talk about crises. Most people going through a crisis want to talk, and they want feedback from the group. Groups need to make this opportunity available. However, some people going through a crisis don't want feedback, so it is important to be sensitive to individual preferences. But it's essential to provide time for crisis sharing. Without it we could mechanically go right into our Bible study and leave people sitting there hurting.

It's important for some sharing to occur early in the evening as in the above story. People come into the group with something on their minds. "I had a fight with my boss." "My child is sick." "Taxes are due next week." People occupied with their own problems won't be able to concentrate on a lesson. Encourage group members to talk over dinner if they're comfortably bonded. If not, it might be best to break up into smaller groups for in-depth sharing before the study.

Breaking the small group into smaller groups of two or three for sharing is important. People today don't know how to relate to each other. When one examines books by writers of an earlier day, such as Charles Dickens and E. M. Forster, it's amazing to see how much time people gave to simply relating to each other back then. People were sensitive to each other even in secular or casual acquaintanceships. In our busyness we've lost that, even in many church circles. One-on-one discussions can help people rediscover this sensitivity.

However, people must be carefully prepared for intimacy. Bonding must take place first, and trust must be developed. To be put into a position of "having" to share can be so threatening to some people that they drop out of the group and refuse to return.

Some groups have found it especially helpful to divide men and women for sharing times. Allen Doran says he has found dividing up by sex to be especially important for men. Women bond easier. Relationships are a life focus for them. Men, however, simply aren't connected to each other. In simpler times past men hunted together and formed relationships that way. Some still go fishing together or play golf, but most men have few relationships with other men, and they have a difficult time relaxing and talking. If men are to be leaders in our culture, they must learn to build relationships with each other.

It is also important to be aware of the fact that there is a sexual element to the intimacy of bonding. Therefore, one-on-one bonding should only be encouraged among group members of the same sex outside the marriage relationship.

Several groups we interviewed said they used to break into small groups or divide men and women for their sharing time, but now that their group is fully bonded they no longer need to do that.

Another important part of the meeting is what happens after it's "over." Significant sharing occurs in the informal time at the end of the evening when everyone is most relaxed.

Whenever it occurs and in whatever kind of group, members are unanimous that sharing is the most important thing. Becki Terral speaks for many: "Our small group is our strongest relationship in the church. We've shared so much in the five years we've been together—physical, emotional, spiritual, financial—we've shared every kind of problem."

PRAYER

◆

Prayer is a natural outgrowth of the sharing time. One small group member said, "Just think how awful it would be if someone shared a really deep need with you, and all you could say was, 'Well, I'm really glad you shared that—I hope talking about it made you feel better. I'll be thinking of you this week. Stay happy, man.' Prayer is such a great privilege. Praying for each other is one of the best things about being a Christian."

Always allow group prayer to be optional, for those who feel led to pray. One author writes,

> Prayer in the small group can be a wonderful or a terrifying experience. People who have never prayed out loud may panic

when told that they are expected to pray, or that prayers will be offered by everyone going around the circle. People who have only heard formal prayers in church may suspect that all prayers must be long, cover many topics, and include a great deal of spiritual language and special phrases. Group prayer under such circumstances and with such expectations can be a most uncomfortable experience.

On the other hand many groups report that the most meaningful part of their life together is the time spent in prayer. In such groups people have learned how to pray with each other, and they find their sense of the presence and power of God enhanced by the group experience. Many small groups carefully allot the last thirty minutes of all meetings for a relaxed, informal time of praying together.[2]

Prayer can be integrated with the sharing by having a volunteer pray immediately after a need or praise has been shared. That adds variety and allows prayer to be connected intimately with what has been shared. It also aids concentration; longer periods of prayer often allow the mind to wander.

The leader sets the example for the prayer time by modeling vulnerability in his sharing and praying. He may pray for the needs that are shared, or he may ask different members of the group to lead in prayer. Usually he will know ahead of time whether or not a certain group member feels comfortable praying before he asks that person to pray in the meeting.

Gene Getz encourages his leaders to follow a prayer pattern using the ACTS acronym in their group prayer times:

Adoration

"Lord, we praise You, we magnify Your name. You alone are worthy of our worship. Bless the Lord, our God Most High."

This important aspect of prayer can carry us into the very courts of the Lord, and by this we fulfill the injunction to "offer up a sacrifice of praise to God, that is, the fruit of lips that give thanks to His name" (Heb. 13:15).

Praising God helps us focus our emotions as well as our intellect on our prayer time. Singing is an excellent way to do this, as is reading the Psalms as a prayer.

Confession

"Almighty and most merciful Father; we have erred, and strayed from thy ways like lost sheep. We have followed too much the devices and desires of our own hearts. We have offended against thy holy laws. We have left undone those things which we ought to have done; and we have done those things which we ought not to have done." So goes the general confession from *The Book of Common Prayer.* It will not be often in small group prayer that such a formal confession will be desired, yet all should approach God with a willingness to confess their faults and the realization that we all fail. Only by confession and forgiveness can our sins be covered, so prayer time should always offer this opportunity.

Thanksgiving

"Be anxious for nothing, but in everything by prayer and supplication with thanksgiving, let your requests be made known to God" (Phil. 4:6).

One of the first things we teach our children is to say thank you, but how often do we forget to thank God for answered prayers and for His many blessings? One of the best ways to remind ourselves of things we need to say thank you for is to keep a list of prayer requests. When we look back at the list of answered prayers, thanksgiving should spring forth automatically.

One group follows a pattern of "high-low" sharing that they learned from the Marriage Encounter movement. When a high, or a praise, is shared for every low, or hurt, we can more readily count our blessings. Then it will be easier to follow the scriptural injunction to "enter His gates with thanksgiving, and His courts with praise. Give thanks to Him; bless His name" (Ps. 100:4).

Supplication

A humble, earnest entreaty of their desires is what God wants to receive from His children. "Ask, and it shall be given to you; seek, and you shall find. . . . For everyone who asks receives, and he who seeks finds." Matthew 7:7 makes clear that far too often in our Christian lives we have not because we ask not. And James adds, "If any of you lacks wisdom, let him ask of God, who gives to all men generously and without reproach, and it will be given to him. But let him ask in faith without any doubting, for the one who doubts is like the surf of the sea driven and tossed by the wind" (1:5-6).

All these—adoration, confession, thanksgiving, and supplication—are central aspects of a balanced prayer life and should be modeled in the small group. Members should also be encouraged to carry them into their own private prayer time. However, certain prayer times may be more focused on one aspect or another. Not every prayer time has to incorporate all four types of prayer. For instance, sometimes it is valuable to spend an evening just adoring God. The leader can instruct everyone to think of something for which to praise God associated with each letter of the alphabet, such as A—God's complete acceptance of us, B—God's beauty, and so on. At other times the needs of the group may be heavy, and an evening spent in supplication will be the appropriate use of your time. Over a period of time, though, a small group should express all four facets in their prayers together.

It can also be helpful to encourage your members to use prayer charts such as this one.

PRAISE REQUESTS   PEOPLE TO PRAY FOR

_____   _____

_____   _____

_____   _____

_____   _____

_____   _____

_____   _____

_____   _____

THINGS TO PRAY ABOUT   ANSWERS TO PRAYER

_____   _____

_____   _____

_____   _____

_____   _____

_____   _____

_____   _____

_____   _____

How to spend thirty minutes in prayer. Divide the time into six 5-minute periods in this order:

| Praise | Confession | Intercession |
| Thanksgiving | Petition | Adoration |

Such charts are helpful for each member to use during his personal devotions and then bring to the small group meetings as a reminder of requests and praises.

Most small groups also have established prayer chains. In some chains each person simply calls the next one on the list with a request. Others have found it more efficient for three or four core couples to be responsible for getting the request to an assigned number of names. That can keep the whole chain from breaking down if someone is out of town or somehow unreachable.

"Using the prayer chain and seeing answered prayer was one of the major factors in getting our group to bond," Becki Terral recalls.

The prayer time at the Flavell group that night was the most meaningful they had ever shared. Mitzi, who had never spoken about her single-parent status or its unique difficulties, brought on a fresh round of sniffling and hugging when she prayed, "Dear God, help me to be a good mother to Lara. Especially help me resist the temptations of men and liquor at my job."

And Susan added a silent prayer of her own. *Thank you, Lord. The miracle has finally happened.*

CHAPTER EIGHT

Ministering in Love

*T*wo days later Susan arrived home from work late with a splitting headache. It had been an exhausting day. She had done a story hour for thirty wiggly kindergartners, struggled to explain the Dewey decimal system to a class of fifth graders who were all dying to get out on the soccer field, and spent two hours with the PTA book committee wrestling over budget limitations and book orders. And she hated getting home late. One of the best parts of working for the school system was that she could be home when Jared and Debbie got home. But today they were already settled into their own activities, and Susan knew those first-flush moments of sharing when they walked in the door could not be recaptured.

And she liked to have dinner on the table when David came home—or at least have something smelling good to greet him. The harder he worked and the more he worried over their debts, the more important she thought it was to have good meals for him. But tonight she was at a loss. She had used the last slice of homemade bread for Jared's sack lunch this morning. They had finished the last can of tuna yesterday. She had some stew in the freezer, but there wasn't time to thaw it out. Her headache was seeping downward to aching neck and shoulders. She wanted to sit down in the middle of the floor and cry—or better yet, go to bed.

But if she did, the problems would still be here when she got up—only magnified because the family would be starving. "Debbie, come set the table when you finish studying those vocabulary words," she called. Well, there was rice to cook, and she could make a batch of biscuits . . . the carrots were a little limp, but they'd add color. She glanced at the clock to see if there would be time to set some lime Jell-O.

Then the doorbell rang. "Jared, can you get that? It's probably one of your friends."

She heard Jared's footsteps going to the door as she put a kettle of water on to boil.

"Mom, I think you'd better come here."

She sighed at Jared's call. If that was a bill collector she really couldn't cope. But it wasn't. "Karen! Tessa! Janice! What are you doing here?" Just the sight of their smiling faces gave her a lift.

"Surprise!" Tessa cried and stepped into the room with a big brown grocery bag in her arms. Karen and Janice followed, each carrying all the groceries they could hold.

"What is this?" Susan felt lightheaded.

"It's called 'turn about's fair play.' Didn't your mother teach you that?" Karen put her bags on the counter and turned to hug Susan. "You and David give us so much in the small group—things we could never repay. You have no idea how much it's helped my marriage just watching you two talk to each other and work together—I'd never seen anything like it before, because my parents were divorced. So we were thrilled when we learned there was *something* we could do for you."

"That's right," Janice added. "You were the very first person who acted like you cared whether we came to church or not—like our family was important. This is how I can say you're important to us too."

"But all this food—it must have cost a hundred dollars—" Susan stopped and just shook her head.

Tessa threw out her arms in her bubbly way. "More, actually—we had a ball! I usually hate grocery shopping, but this was a party. We've all got problems, but money just doesn't happen to be one of ours, so we can help you with this the same way you help us in areas you don't have problems— like showing us a really happy Christian family. I thought that was just storybook stuff until we got to know you guys in the small group."

Karen was busy emptying the sacks and putting items in the refrigerator. "What are you having for dinner? Shall I leave these steaks out for tonight?"

When David came home an hour later Susan and Debbie were both wearing fresh dresses and candles were flickering on the table. "What is this? I thought we didn't believe in playing the lottery."

Between bites of succulent T-bones Susan told David what had happened. "Oh, and I almost forgot to tell you— Karen said business is going crazy at her boutique—people have started Christmas shopping already. She offered Jared a job delivering packages on Saturday afternoons, and I can do gift wrapping for her whenever I have time."

She smiled at her family enjoying their dinner. "I know this is simply another example of God providing—as He always does. But what really amazes me is that my whole goal in this small group thing was to minister to *other* people—and look how they've ministered to us!"

David nodded. "I know. We've got an awful lot to learn, don't we?"

DOING GOOD
◆

Ministering by taking meals to needy members, mowing lawns for sick members, and celebrating with fortunate members is all an extension of sharing. Someone has called such activities "the small group on wheels."

Taking food to families in stressful situations is a frequent "outside ministry." Just as eating together in the small group is of primary importance, so sharing food is one of the best ways to provide emotional support, whether there is death or illness in the family or a joyful occasion such as moving into a new house or having a family reunion. When Jesus told Peter to "feed My sheep," He surely meant with physical as well as spiritual food.

Providing meals is a small group function that the leader may need to organize initially, but someone else can soon take on that ministry as his or her special contribution to the group. You will need a method for organizing this activity. On the next page is a form that Gene Getz's church uses.

In other situations it might be best simply to take in bags of groceries, as the Flavell's small group did, or to provide one meal a day with people signing up to provide salad, main dish, or dessert. Whatever your method, the love that is expressed through the food and the contact with those who bring it will be an important contribution to the kingdom of Christ, our Servant King.

SMALL GROUP MEAL SUPPORT FUNCTION

◆

Meals Needed For: _____

Address: _____ Phone # _____

Sunday ___ / ___ / ___   Monday ___ / ___ / ___
Breakfast _____   Breakfast _____
Lunch _____   Lunch _____
Dinner _____   Dinner _____

Tuesday ___ / ___ / ___   Wednesday ___ / ___ / ___
Breakfast _____   Breakfast _____
Lunch _____   Lunch _____
Dinner _____   Dinner _____

Thursday ___ / ___ / ___   Friday ___ / ___ / ___
Breakfast _____   Breakfast _____
Lunch _____   Lunch _____
Dinner _____   Dinner _____

Saturday ___ / ___ / ___
Breakfast _____
Lunch _____
Dinner _____

Visiting hospitals and sick rooms is another important area of ministry, not only for the support that can be demonstrated but also for the doors it can open. One example of this was Marie, who had been abused by her uncles and cousins when she was a child. She had never been able to open up and share that pain at a small group meeting. Then she was hospitalized for an appendectomy. When her small group leaders visited her in the hospital, she was suddenly able to open up to them. That night began the healing of much more than Marie's abdomen.

As we have seen in the story of the Flavells, business crises provide another area for ministry. Jim and Becki Terral tell the story of their Christian bookstore to illustrate how their small group ministered to them. "It was when the recession hit Dallas—hard. We were among the many who suddenly found themselves unemployed, so we opened a small Christian book business in our living room."

"The Lord blessed that amazingly," Becki recalled. "Pretty soon the way opened up to move our business from our home to a store."

Jim shook his head. "Only trouble was, I was sick—flat on my back. We didn't know what we were going to do. The opportunity seemed too great to let it go, but there was no way Becki could move all that herself."

"Then our small group came to the rescue. They built and painted shelves, picked up supplies, stocked shelves. The whole store became an extension of the small group.

"And there was the matter of the light fixtures. There we were with just bare bulbs and no money to buy fixtures. They looked worse every time I noticed them, especially when the store was freshly painted and the shelves arranged so nicely—there were these awful bulbs hanging from wires. A fellow in our congregation heard about our need. He worked for a department store that had changed its decor. Just that week his boss had told him to get rid of their old light fixtures."

Becki smiled. "The night before our grand opening was one of the most precious memories of my life. We had a dedication service here with our whole small group. And Jim was feeling fine by then, too."

One of the most difficult situations can be long-term illnesses. Tom and Tiffany were the all-American couple. He was captain of the football team; she was homecoming queen. They got married, had successful careers and a beautiful family. They were one of the strongest couples in their small group—the ones everyone else leaned on for support.

Then they discovered Tiffany had a brain tumor. Suddenly their resources were gone. Allen Doran will never forget the evening Tom—6 feet, 2 inches, 290 pounds of muscle—broke down and cried in their group.

The women set up a schedule for taking their two girls to music lessons and parties and doing Tiffany's shopping for her. The men took turns taking Tom out to lunch or coffee. The group was there for them day and night.

Fortunately, that story had a happy ending because Tiffany responded beautifully to chemotherapy and was completely healed. Now they're back ministering to others from the strength they gained through that experience.

But not all such stories are so successful. Helen told us about a situation her small group is going through right now. "Betty was one of the most active and self-sufficient people I've ever met. When she wasn't working at her real estate business, she was out walking or playing volleyball. And she didn't even have to work—her husband is a top executive for IBM, but she said she didn't like to ask him for money; she wanted to do it herself.

"Then she came down with a particularly crippling form of arthritis. She couldn't accept the disease, and she couldn't accept our support. At every small group sharing time she'd tell us how mad she was at God. We wanted to do something for her to show her we cared, so three of us women called and made an appointment to go over and clean her house for her. When we got there she'd already cleaned it herself.

"We are learning a lot from this. We've seen the importance of being open and loving and praying for her—and the importance of waiting. We know not to try counseling or helping until she's ready for it. Our small group leader says he's learning to deal with the situation, and he feels he'll mature through the experience—as we all will."

One small group member urges, "Don't just go to church, don't just go to a meeting. Find a group you can identify with, and share the joy of helping others. That's Christianity in action; that's the small group."

DEALING WITH PAIN
♦

One of the major issues small group leaders and members alike face is pain. It is inevitable; life is painful. One of the most rampant myths in America today, and especially among Christians, is the idea that people shouldn't hurt. Pain is always present in a group—even more so than in the same number of individuals, because when one person in a group picks up on something it is magnified and reflected by the others in the group. The question is whether the group deals with pain in healthy or unhealthy ways. The better a group deals with pain, the better the group members will be able to serve each other.

It is important to keep in mind two principles for dealing with hurt in a group. First, acknowledge that Christians hurt. Pain is not always the direct result of sin (other than the fact that we live in a fallen world). That realization should remove any spiritual guilt attached to the pain.

Second, realize that people can be happy in spite of pain. That is especially true in a small group, because much happiness comes from a sense of community. Isolated people have the most trouble with pain.

Beware of unhealthy ways of dealing with pain; don't magnify it. Hurt is bad enough as it is, but a spark can easily be fanned into a flame by an overreacting group.

Also, don't let the pain of one person disable the group. If one member is demanding so much love and attention that the group can't fulfill those needs, that person needs to be placed in the care of a counselor.

When confronted by suffering in the group, pray for the person or the situation immediately. Don't just say, "We'll put this on our prayer list," or even wait until the scheduled prayer time in the group. If someone is bleeding he needs a bandage right away.

Also accept the fact that people are in pain. Don't try to argue them out of it—even if the situation doesn't sound terribly painful to you. Don't belittle a person's hurt. Be sure, however, that your reactions are honest. If you don't understand, say so. You can say, "I don't really know what you're going through, but I love you." Above all, don't say, "I know how you feel," if you don't.

Listen to the person and love him. Don't try to give advice, and don't quote Scripture as a slick solution. Saying, "In all things give thanks," or, "All things work together for good," as pat answers will only make the person mad.

On the other hand, sharing comforting Scriptures in a loving manner can be very meaningful. A good example is the first chapter of 2 Corinthians, which includes verses 3-5: "Blessed be the God and Father of our Lord Jesus Christ, the Father of mercies and God of all comfort; who comforts us in all our affliction so that we may be able to comfort those who are in any affliction with the comfort with which we ourselves are comforted by God. For just as the sufferings of Christ are ours in abundance, so also our comfort is abundant through Christ." Others are: Psalm 23, Philippians 4:6-7, Romans 8:23 *and following* to the end of the chapter, which says, "For I am convinced that neither death, nor life, nor angels, nor principalities, nor things present, nor things to come, nor powers, nor height, nor depth, nor any other created thing, shall be able to separate us from the love of God, which is in Christ Jesus our Lord."

People in distress don't need sermons; they need to be taken seriously. A woman in a small group was suffering from a very painful jaw disorder. When she had finished sharing, a man in the group said, "If there's anything I hate, it's a complaining woman."

If something like that happens in a group, the offending member must be taken aside by the leader. "You hurt her feelings," his leader told him. The amazing thing was that the man didn't have any idea he had hurt her. He was really sorry and went immediately to apologize.

Nancy, another small group member, recalls the night a woman in their group returned to their group after being in a mental hospital for sixty days. "She had been severely abused as a child and was suicidal. She was still in counseling, still struggling, but making progress. She very timidly shared a little of this with our group.

"We were all quiet when she finished. I don't think any of us knew the right thing to say, but we recognized the *wrong* thing when somebody said, 'Well, you'll just have to turn it over to the Lord.'" Of course the Lord could help her, but that woman needed in-depth help, not some of the "have a nice day" variety.

Gene Getz says he learned a lot about how to reach hurting people when he had an open line radio talk show in the Dallas area. He soon learned that more hurting people called if he wasn't overly cheerful and breezy. He needed to use a quiet, soft approach. If you want people to speak out of their pain, you must first learn to be comfortable with silence and give people time to speak or pray. You can also prime someone ahead of time—ask him or her before the meeting, "Would you like to tell your story?" Or you can throw out a question to get the sharing started. Gene Getz learned to ask questions such as, "How have you struggled with your faith?" Then he'd play a song to give people time to think. He'd come back and ask, "What's on your mind? If it's something current maybe you need our prayers now."

Groups struggling with painful situations might want to tailor their study time around that. A study of the Scriptures listed above could be helpful, or studying books such as C. S. Lewis's *The Problem of Pain,* Philip Yancey's *Where Is God When It Hurts?*, or Yancey's *Disappointment with God* can help the hurting member and give the others understanding that will help them be supportive.

GROUP DYNAMICS
◆

Earlier we looked at the question, What can a leader do to speed up the bonding process? Besides getting to know the people in the group and modeling openness and acceptance, he also needs to understand group dynamics and how to apply certain discussion techniques to the small group. *How to Lead Small Groups,* by Navpress, and *Leading Small Groups,* by InterVarsity Press, are helpful handbooks on this topic.

Although the person with a healthy self-concept is basically the same person whether alone or in a group, his outward behavior and responses will vary according to those around him. The small group leader needs to be aware of this fact and be prepared to cope with various situations that may arise.

People will be most themselves when they are relaxed; therefore it is the duty of the leader to see to the physical comfort and arrangement of the room—seating, lighting, temperature—to the extent possible. You will achieve the best group response if everyone is on an equal seating level, for example, so it is best to have all chairs arranged so that no one has to sit on the floor or on a high stool.

The three vital experiences of a small group are: learning experiences, relational experiences, and witnessing experiences. All three can best be enhanced through meaningful group discussions. A small group discussion should be viewed simply as an enlarged conversation—not as a public speaking or panel discussion situation. The purpose of your discussion may vary from meeting to meeting. Sometimes you will want the group merely to visit and get better acquainted, to speed the bonding process; sometimes you will want to pool knowledge and help the group or individuals find answers to situations or apply scriptural teachings; sometimes you will want to provide an atmosphere where group members can be heard because they need someone to talk to. The leader needs to be sensitive to the needs of the group because their needs won't always match his pre-planned ideas.

Whatever the purposes, however, the time will be spent most successfully if all members can be encouraged to obey the basic rules of any group discussion: be relevant, be brief, be courteous, and be cooperative.

And the general rules for the leader of any group discussion are the same:

- Open the discussion with a brief statement or question.
- Keep the discussion moving by asking questions.
- Give all members of the group an equal opportunity to talk.
- Don't take a position as leader; encourage other members to do so.
- Watch time limits.
- Close with a brief summarizing statement.

Your group discussions will be more stimulating if lots of people participate. Larger group discussions are often more energetic and adventurous. The larger the group, however, the higher the anxiety level will be for some members. There will also be more likelihood of heightened emotional responses.

Questions are one of the leader's most valuable tools. Many techniques can serve to guide the discussion. Two of the most valuable are those used to restrain the talkative and to encourage the reticent.

If someone is dominating the group discussion the leader should not look at him, as that encourages communication. Instead, interrupt with a question such as, "Judy, may I interrupt here to ask how the group feels about your idea?" or, "Mark, what do you think of Judy's idea?"

To encourage the reticent try to seat them where it will be easy for the leader to maintain eye contact. Whenever they venture to make a remark respond to them with nodded head, a smile, or some body language to let them know they are being heard. Such questions as, "That's a good point, Jane—can you tell us more about it?" or, "Sam, you look like you're thinking hard—do you want to add something?" will often draw out the shy member.

If you think someone wants to share but doesn't speak in the group, or if a person seems to be rejecting the group by sitting with arms folded and head down, that person can often benefit from a talk with the leader alone. Perhaps you can walk out to the car with him or her and ask, "Did something happen this week?" "Is something bothering you about the group?" "Can I help you with something?" The key to helping a reticent person is not confronting him in the group but nurturing him.

Occasionally certain groups within the group will do all the talking while others will be silent, such as women out-talking the men, or younger members dominating the discussions while older members remain quiet. Allen Doran does not recommend pointing out such a situation by saying, "The men seem to be doing all the talking. What do you women think?" Instead, he recommends that you divide the group up, and ask them privately, "I've noticed the more mature group here is awfully quiet. Do you have any clues to what's going on?"

The better people know each other the more comfortable they will feel about asking questions that are important to them and expressing opinions they really mean. Two simple techniques can help speed this process: name tags and get-acquainted forms. Many people block even on well-known names. For this reason we strongly recommend regular use of name tags. The leader should also use names as often as possible to help the group learn them. If you can't read someone's name tag, don't be afraid to ask. The leader should set the pattern by feeling free to do this.

Get-acquainted forms should be filled out by every member at the first meeting and updated frequently. Many groups find it helpful to photocopy the sheets and staple them together so that every member can have a copy. The sheets should include such information as:

> Name
> Address
> Phone Number
> Age
> Occupation
> Family Members, Ages of Children
> Formerly Lived
> Attended School
> Hobbies
> Favorite Books, Games, Songs, Sports
> Birthday
> Anniversary
> Favorite Color, Food
> Dreams
> Things I Want You to Know About Me
> Things I Don't Want You to Know About Me

Give people plenty of room to write, and don't be afraid to introduce frivolous subjects—you often learn the most about a person that way, and when two group members discover a shared passion for origami you'll have immediate bonding.

You will find that people gravitate to certain issues in life; likewise, a group gravitates to certain issues as topics come up. One couple or person within the group will be more sensitive in certain areas than in others and so will be drawn to that subject and give advice on it—thereby enriching the group. Encourage people to develop and share their specialities. When someone raises a specific issue or question in the group discussion it is likely that someone in the group will be able to respond to that person. Then you have true communication and sharing—a primary goal of the small group.

To help each member of your group participate more fully you might want to distribute a group membership exercise. The following is designed to help group members and leaders think about their role in the group and see how they can function more effectively.

UNDERSTANDING YOUR GROUP BEHAVIOR

Each of the following items describes a group behavior. In the space next to each item write 5 if you *always* behave that way, 4 if you *frequently* behave that way, 3 if you *occasionally* behave that way, 2 if you *seldom* behave that way, and 1 if you *never* behave that way.

When I am a member of a group:

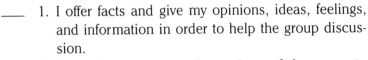

____ 1. I offer facts and give my opinions, ideas, feelings, and information in order to help the group discussion.

____ 2. I warmly encourage all members of the group to participate. I am open to their ideas; I let them know I value their contributions to the group.

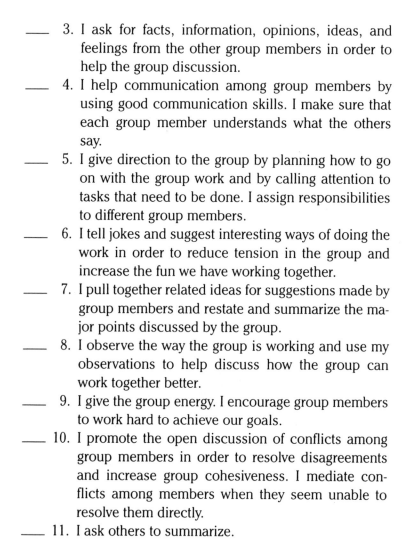

_____ 3. I ask for facts, information, opinions, ideas, and feelings from the other group members in order to help the group discussion.

_____ 4. I help communication among group members by using good communication skills. I make sure that each group member understands what the others say.

_____ 5. I give direction to the group by planning how to go on with the group work and by calling attention to tasks that need to be done. I assign responsibilities to different group members.

_____ 6. I tell jokes and suggest interesting ways of doing the work in order to reduce tension in the group and increase the fun we have working together.

_____ 7. I pull together related ideas for suggestions made by group members and restate and summarize the major points discussed by the group.

_____ 8. I observe the way the group is working and use my observations to help discuss how the group can work together better.

_____ 9. I give the group energy. I encourage group members to work hard to achieve our goals.

_____ 10. I promote the open discussion of conflicts among group members in order to resolve disagreements and increase group cohesiveness. I mediate conflicts among members when they seem unable to resolve them directly.

_____ 11. I ask others to summarize.

The functioning of a group will be enhanced if every member clearly understands what is expected of him. In order to help their members, Richard Meier's group has nine stated norms in printed form that are distributed to all new members, reviewed verbally occasionally in the group, and modeled regularly by group members and leaders.

1. Families arrange their own baby-sitting.
2. Be on time for all meetings.
3. Respect confidentiality.
4. Attend meetings regularly.
5. Share meaningful aspects of ourselves.
6. Respect and listen to one another without interruption.
7. Use the Bible as the ultimate standard of truth.
8. Allow the church doctrinal statement to be the final source of appeal on differences of interpretation.
9. Differ with one another, but with respect; confront one another, but with love.

They do well on all the rules, they report, except number six. They often get carried away with discussion and interrupt each other, but it's partly a sign of how well they've bonded that they feel so free to exchange ideas. If they find someone making an erroneous application of a biblical truth, the leader puts it back to the group to ask for more information.

CHAPTER NINE

Understanding Each Other

*D*avid closed his Bible and leaned back with a sigh. He couldn't remember when he'd enjoyed guiding a lesson more. Maybe because he so thoroughly believed in God's guidance in the Christian life and because it was such a constant desire of his own heart never to step outside of that guidance that the study had come straight from his heart. And the entire group had responded warmly as they considered Proverbs 3:5-6: "Trust in the Lord with all your heart, and do not lean on your own understanding. In all your ways acknowledge Him, and He will make your paths straight."

David had introduced the text by having the group sing the beautiful old hymn "Saviour, Like a Shepherd Lead Us," and they had done a responsive reading of the Twenty-third Psalm, with the men and women reading alternate verses. Then, following the three-part approach to Bible study, David had directed the group's attention to the four parts of the text. He thought he had sensed more spiritual growth in their reflective responses as they defined trusting in the Lord and leaning not on their own understanding than he had seen in any previous study. And when they moved on to define how they could acknowledge Him in all their ways and how He directs their paths, David felt like a proud parent at an awards assembly—many of the group's insights exceeded his own.

Reflecting on it all later with Susan, he declared, "Yes, I was happy—proud of them, even. But surely it wasn't spiritual pride—the kind the Bible says goes before a fall—I wasn't proud of anything *I* had done; rather, I was humbled by how far they had outstripped me.

"But, Susan, how could anything that started out so right go so suddenly wrong? What did I do? Or what did I not do? I'm afraid to go back—what if everything blows up in my face like that again? Ev always seemed to be such a quiet, agreeable sort—what did I do to set him off like that? And then Alex—she's always so cheerful—suddenly bursting into tears like that—I don't know. Do you think they'll come back? Do you think *anyone* will come back?"

Susan shook her head, not knowing what to say, as they both relived the ugly scene in their minds. It was during the third stage of the study, where group members were encouraged to respond personally to the passage, that David had asked, "What is one decision facing you that you find difficult, and why?" Susan had mentioned her own feelings of inadequacy in trying to help her children select the right classes for school and how difficult that was when she didn't know what God wanted each child to do in the future. One of the men had talked about a business decision—something about whether his company should merge with another, but he hadn't been too specific.

"And then I looked at Ev," David said. "I didn't mean to be singling him out—I wouldn't do that—my eye just happened to catch his—and all of a sudden he was yelling."

Susan shivered at the memory. "I know. I never really could figure out what he was saying. I think he made a decision once based on what he thought was God's will, and everything went terribly wrong."

David nodded. "That's what I thought he was saying, but I couldn't figure out whether he was mad at me for bringing the subject up or at the group for discussing it or at God for letting him down."

"Maybe he was mad at himself for making a mistake. And then Alex—was she upset for Ev's sake or about something in her own life?" Susan shook her head. "Where do we go from here?"

David spread out his hands helplessly. "I think I should enroll in a college course in psychology."

PERSONALITY STYLES

◆

It isn't really necessary to get a graduate degree in psychology, but at some time all small group leaders, like David, are going to feel woefully inadequate when faced with the variety of human personalities. Your introduction to personality styles may not be as dramatic or stressful as David's, but it is essential to understand the way different personality types react to situations. There are eight common personality styles most likely to be encountered in a small group. The better we understand one another, the better we can minister to one another.

The Perfectionistic Person

The perfectionistic person is logical, usually intelligent, and high in the cognitive area of the SOI Questionnaire (see Appendix A). He is not, however, closely in touch with his feelings. He believes that being correct is more important than feeling good. A perfectionist wants the small group to study systematic theology and all of its historical applications. He contributes greatly to the education of the group but needs to be drawn into the process of applying his knowledge. He resists psychological and practical application. The small group leader should draw him out by reflecting his feelings back to him.

Perfectionists tend to be the oldest child of their sex in a family. They are usually successful people but are also very anxious. A perfectionist personality has great capacity for organization and detail and can get a lot accomplished. The danger, however, is that growth will not take place in a perfectionistic routine because of a lack of relational application. Pride is also a danger for this personality type, as is legalism. A legalistic perfectionist sees weaknesses in his neighbors but not in himself. The group leader needs to help him respect and accommodate others' faults.

The perfectionist personality can be modeled after the apostle Paul—the man dedicated to eradicating error. God used Paul as a great theologian but also taught him the importance of caring about people.

The Emotional Person

The emotional person can be styled after the apostle Peter—the one who "let it all hang out." The apostle Peter was vulnerable and feeling-oriented but usually not logical. This person is most often a middle child and will score high in the relational area of the SOI index.

Emotional people are able to share their feelings readily and are helpful in the bonding process of the group. An individual of this personality type, however, usually has holes in his soul from being a middle child and never having his parents' total attention. Therefore he may want to dominate the group by doing all the talking. It's not unusual for an emotional person to pray for half or more of the entire time allotted.

If this problem occurs in a group, the emotional person must be confronted, or he will never grow. The leader should take him aside and speak the truth in love. "You might want to work on developing your listening skills" is often a diplomatic approach. It is also helpful to try to get the emotional person to talk about facts rather than always focusing on feelings. If the leader doesn't deal with an overly emotional person, the group will either fall apart, or they will confront the individual as a group, which can be very hurtful.

The Secretive Person

The secretive person doesn't trust people, usually because he was put down by parents or others as a child. Often he grew up with repressed anger and mistrust. This type of person wants to control the decision making in the group— where to eat, what to study, how often to meet, and so on. He likely exhibits perfectionistic characteristics, such as shying away from personal application studies. He prefers "safe" subjects, such as doctrinal issues. This person may be hostile toward the leader, whom he sees as a threat because authority figures in his childhood were abusive.

The secretive person does not bond or share easily. He thinks, *If I share that, they'll use it to hurt me.* Secretive people need a great deal of support when they do disclose something. It is important not to speculate beyond what he shares; just pray for whatever need he identifies. That builds trust.

Remember that this kind of person is secretive, suspicious, and sometimes hostile because he has been severely hurt in his youth. The group must love him and try to get him to talk about his feelings. That takes a great deal of patience, but keep reaching out, even when he is abrupt. Secretive people usually have low social skills, and their feelings are hurt easily. When a secretive person works through his feelings and forgives the person who hurt him, however, he will become one of the most sensitive people in the group. He will have a sort of radar to others' hurts because of his own.

The Dependent Person

The dependent person was usually the youngest child in a family, and his parents made most of his choices for him. A dependent personality is most often an underachiever. He comes late to meetings, makes commitments but doesn't keep them, and refuses to vote but then gripes about the decision. A dependent person often plays "poor me" in the sharing time. He wants specific instructions as to what he should do about his problems, but then he argues with the one giving advice or later says that it didn't work. This person has a subconscious goal to make the leader fail, because he sees it as a means of getting even with authority figures.

A group leader can help a dependent person gain insights into his background, and the dependent can grow out of his unhealthy habits once he is aware of his problem. When dealing with a dependent, it's very important never to give direct advice. If the person asks for advice say, "What are your options? What do you think you ought to do?"

He will say, "I don't know."

The group can be steered to help him do his own thinking by asking questions such as, "What do you think God wants you to do?" "What does the Bible say?"

Then direct the person to make a list. Guide him to make a choice. "Which looks the best to you? Where do you want to start?"

When the person has made a choice, compliment his decision and summon group support. "We'll pray for you this week while you try that. We're all proud of you."

The dependent may not carry through or may sabotage his own plan. The leader should hold him accountable. If the person says the plan didn't work ask, "What's your plan B?" Always be supportive, and give hearty compliments for good results.

The Shy Person

The shy person was generally not given enough physical stimulation in early life; he was often a bottle-fed baby who needed more hugs than he received and was not given enough freedom to express his feelings. Such a person will be taking a big risk in joining a small group because of his fears of close groups and his fears of rejection. Once he makes the decision to join, however, he will be loyal to the group. Shy people make strong commitments.

A shy person is afraid of anger. He may have grown up in a family where abusive words were hurled frequently or even may have suffered physical attack. On the other hand, he might have grown up in such a sheltered environment that he never encountered harshness until later in life and had no defenses for dealing with it. Either way, this kind of personality avoids confrontation at all costs. He may want to express himself, but it will come out very meekly and he will only say part of what he wanted to.

Shy people are usually intelligent, responsible, and mature. But they need to be handled gently. It is the job of the leader to draw out the shy individual. Encourage him to share his feelings, support him, make him feel safe, let him know that his feelings are important by listening carefully to whatever he expresses. This is a person your group can really help to grow. He can be brought out in a safe environment if given the opportunity. Think of your shy member as a beautiful garden flower: if you tend to his needs, he'll bloom for you.

The Explosive Person

The explosive person is usually very nice and goes out of his way to help others. Most of the time he is calm and pleasant and does not express hurt or anger. He does, however, keep track of wrongs subconsciously, and the kettle simmers, building up steam under the lid. Some minor decision of the group brings on a sudden explosion that shocks everybody. You will recognize this personality type in Ev, who suddenly erupted in the middle of the Flavell small group.

Try to get an explosive person to share his or her anger and frustrations little by little. When the rest of the group is upset, this person is at his calmest outwardly. Try to allow him to vent his feelings with the group then, rather than letting them simmer until a later explosion. Encourage verbalizing anger in the group, always with "I" statements: "I feel that . . . " "I am mad about . . . " Never allow name-calling or verbal attacks, such as, "You are . . . " Encourage the explosive person to realize that anger is not sin, but it must be dealt with. "Be angry, and yet do not sin; do not let the sun go down on your anger" (Eph. 4:26). Your group might want to do a study of Matthew 5:23-26 on Christ's instructions for dealing with anger against a brother.

Sometimes, however, an explosive style can be simply a matter of cultural origin rather than a disorder from unresolved anger. You may have a "hot-blooded Italian" in a group of "proper Englishmen." This is not to belittle either of those nationalities but to point out differences of style and background. Some groups find such differences stimulating and grow from them. If, however, this mix is disabling your group, the leader might need to take the overly expressive person aside and say, "Your emphatic eruptions are making the group uncomfortable. Do you think you might want to soften your expressions a little?"

The High/Low Person

Extreme personality changes can be evidence of a metabolic disorder. One percent of the population needs medication to control emotional swings. If a leader suspects this is the case, he should speak to the person and recommend that he see a doctor.

Alex, who most often exhibited a top-of-the-world attitude to her small group and then suddenly burst into tears one night at a tense moment in Bible study is one example of this personality type, although it exhibits itself in many forms.

Milder mood shifts that don't stem from a medical problem may also occur in a group member. If someone in your group is sometimes emotional and aggressive—a real bulldozer—but at other times withdrawn, shy, and quiet, the leader should also speak to him privately. Reflect to him what you see. "This is what I've noticed in the group . . . "

The high/low person is ecstatic one week but has "lost his salvation" the next. One week he moans, "Why did I ever trust that person?" The next week when you ask about the problem, he won't remember it. "Oh, I made it up." Everything for him is the experience of the moment. The problem in the group is that he loses credibility, so he needs a great deal of tolerance. Try to react calmly to whichever mood he is in at the moment. This person gets a great deal of satisfaction from sharing, so encourage him to do so as long as it isn't disruptive to the group.

If the high/low person talks about his mood shifts with the group, it can be very helpful for the group to reflect back to him what they see. The group must be loving. Accept him, help him calm down when he's pushy, and draw him out when he's shy. Developing sensitivity within the group and an attitude of loving support will benefit the other members as much as the one being helped. In extreme cases, hospitalization by a Christian psychiatrist may be needed to regulate severe mood swings with medication, followed by lifelong mental health checkups.

The Antisocial Person

The antisocial person is extremely self-centered and is therefore the hardest to work with in a group. He sees people as objects to be used. If the small group goes out to eat, he leaves the tab for someone else; he uses the small group for business purposes; if there is a slight sickness at home, he wants meals brought in. The needs of an antisocial person are a bottomless pit because his continual question is, "What can the group do for me?"

We are all born that way. Infants are selfish and demanding and expect the world to revolve around them. But through discipline, love, education, and good role models, most of us outgrow our selfishness to a certain degree. The antisocial person is still immature. He is the person the writer of Proverbs had in mind when he wrote, "A child who gets his own way brings shame to his mother" (Prov. 29:15). The antisocial person usually grew up without discipline, but some were severely abused as children.

This person can be dangerous because he probably has a great deal of charisma. People of this personality type make effective con artists. In a small group he tries to dominate. He may try to have an affair with another's spouse in the group because he has a sense of entitlement to whatever will gratify him for the moment.

Be careful with this type of person, but give him a chance. Confront him privately, ask him not to dominate the group, hold him accountable, and pray for him. It will not be easy for him to change, but try to create a desire in him to overcome his problem. If he really wants to grow, teach him Philippians 4:13: "I can do all things through [Christ] who strengthens me."

It is possible that this person will grow, but it is more likely that he will quit. The leader and group members need to be aware of this likelihood so they won't be overly upset if he does leave the group.

KNOWING WHEN TO REFER

Although helping people with a variety of personality styles will help your group grow and most people will respond to love, patience, and careful handling, someone in your group may need more help than loving friends and informed laymen can give. He or she may need to be referred to a professional Christian therapist.

Five indicators show when an individual should be referred to a professional.

1. Refer anyone who is suicidal, including severely depressed individuals.
2. Refer anyone who is homicidal.
3. Refer anyone with an obvious physical problem.
4. Refer anyone who cannot be handled adequately because of limited time in the leader's schedule.
5. Refer anyone with a problem beyond the leader's ability to handle or that the leader feels uncomfortable handling.

Also watch for anyone in the group whose thoughts are regularly disconnected, cannot express himself coherently, or cannot follow the expressed thoughts of others.

Richard Meier even suggests the possibility of administering a personality profile to potential group members to see if someone is more suited to a counseling or twelve-step group. A preliminary weeding-out process would prevent the disruption of a whole group by one individual who needs more help than the group can give. It would also be a means for the individual to get focused help quickly. However, Gene Getz expresses the concern that such procedures would have to be administered very carefully to avoid unnecessarily intimidating sensitive potential leaders and members. Large churches should offer special support groups for individuals in serious need, such as dealing with death and dying, divorce recovery, and alcohol recovery.

Just the fact that you might have referred someone to professional counseling, however, should not automatically remove him from the group. People in counseling need a group they can come to where everything doesn't revolve around them and their problem as it would in Alcoholics Anonymous, Overeaters Anonymous, or any of the twelve-step groups. This way the small group ministry can continue on a less intense level, which will undoubtedly be a relief to all.

PROJECTION

———◆———

In this chapter, which focuses on meeting human needs, especially psychological needs, we need to discuss one last factor. Projection is the dynamic that is evident when Judy says, "I don't like what Jim does. I don't know why I don't like it. He just gets on my nerves." The number one cause of such a feeling is that Jim is doing something that Judy does and dislikes in herself.

Projection is what Christ is talking about in Matthew 7:3: "Why do you look at the speck that is in your brother's eye, but do not notice the log that is in your own eye?" According to Paul Meier, when you put your hand on an overhead projection, you see a huge hand on the screen. But the hand is really on the projector. This is projection. It's a defense mechanism that we all use at times.

If you have unconscious anger toward yourself, you will project it to someone who reminds you of yourself. You will hypocritically preach to that person, have trouble accepting that person, and have trouble loving him until you realize that the little bit of rage or lust or greed or whatever it is you see in him reminds you a *whole bunch* of the same thing you don't want to see in yourself.

It is important for the leader to listen carefully to someone who may be projecting. If the problem continues, he should try to draw him or her out in private conversation. Help Judy see that Jim isn't the problem at all, rather it's her own feelings, and then help her really get to know Jim through sharing and prayer. That will usually take care of the problem.

It is important to remember that leaders can also be guilty of projection. It's not even unusual from the pulpit. The key is to watch for a theme—is a leader or group member forever harping on a single issue? If so, that person should ask himself: What am I struggling with? Am I sharing something meaningful? Am I too emotional? Am I using this as a rationalization? Am I using this as a smoke screen? An example might be someone who forever talks about the sin of immorality yet is lusting after his neighbor's wife.

A comment one sometimes hears is, "There wouldn't be so much counseling going on if the churches were doing their job." In reality, the reverse is true. The better job our churches do, the more hurts and needs we'll uncover, and the more counseling we'll be called on to give.

Occasionally someone objects to growth groups as being "too psychological." As an argument against the need for psychological understanding and counseling, such a person will usually quote 2 Peter 1:3-4:

> His divine power has granted to us everything pertaining to life and godliness, through the true knowledge of Him who called us by His own glory and excellence. For by these He has granted to us His precious and magnificent promises, in order that by them you might become partakers of the divine nature, having escaped the corruption that is in the world by lust.

In reality, the original Greek words in that passage imply that an intimate relationship (*epignoseos*—"full knowledge") with Christ is our source of spiritual growth and power (*dynameos*) to develop spiritual vitality (*eusebeian*). This passage has absolutely nothing to do with our need for psychotherapy for emotional problems or medication for physical problems. People who are afraid to examine their own psychology (as the apostle Paul instructs us to do in Galatians 6:4) resist groups and tend to be superspiritual, "holier than thou," and immature. They will also take Scripture verses out of context to fight growth groups in the church. Satan has always been a wolf in sheep's clothing.

Such rejection of help, however, is unbiblical. Jesus said sick people need doctors. If God enables scientists to discover something that benefits mankind, such as penicillin or insulin, we should tell Him thank you and then use it for His glory.

The challenge of understanding people and their interactions in a group in order to reach out and minister to them in love is one of the greatest challenges of the Christian life. If we are to function as Christ's hands and feet in the Body of Christ, it is an inescapable duty and more—it is a prized opportunity that God has given us.

CHAPTER TEN

Coping with Success

*D*avid Flavell took his seat around the long, dark-wood conference table in the church board room. Although he smiled outwardly and returned pleasantries to his fellow elders, inwardly he struggled to shift gears. Uncle Clarence had had a heart attack the day after Christmas. Now he was staying with David and Susan to convalesce. And welcome as he was, that did mean another mouth to feed—not to mention the doctor bills that he would probably need help with. If only Flavell Construction could have been first rather than second on that bid on the convenience store today. It was a small job, but it would have kept the family going, even if it wouldn't have been enough to pay off any of their debts. And the townhouse remodeling project that had kept them in macaroni and peanut butter the past nine months was completed now. *Where next, God?* David wondered.

Then, David suddenly became aware that Pastor Tudway was directing the same question to the board. Bethany Bible Church had now had its small group program operational for a full year. There had been many successes and many problems. Some of the old problems had been solved, and some new ones had emerged. And now they must ask, "Where next, God?"

Pastor Tudway stood in front of a big blackboard, holding a long piece of yellow chalk poised to write. "I want us to brainstorm on this. Just throw out to me all the things we've accomplished this year as fast as you think of them."

The items came faster than he could write.

"Twenty small groups formed."

"Almost fifty percent of our congregation in small groups."

"Groups growing."

"New people wanting to join."

"Sixteen new church members by profession of faith."

"Teen program emphasizing groups bursting at the seams."

"People comfortable in small groups."

"Lots of ministering."

The list went on until the board was covered, and Pastor Tudway had to stop and shake the circulation back into his hand. A couple of members got up to refill their coffee cups.

"Now," the pastor called them back to order and turned the blackboard over. "Let's list our problems."

Again the answers came faster than he could write.

"Some people have dropped out."

"We have some discouraged leaders."

"Small groups growing too big."

"People having to wait to join."

"Need more seating space in sanctuary."

"Teen center too small."

"People too comfortable."

"Some leaders nearing burnout."

And again the list went on until the board was covered.

When they finished and compared their two lists, everyone laughed in surprise. It was easy to see that their successes had caused their problems. Pastor Tudway smiled. "Since the small group approach has been so successful, I want to apply it to this situation." He divided the board members into five small groups and assigned a problem area to each one. They were to return in a month with suggested solutions. David smiled wryly when the pastor appointed his group to study attrition. *Well, I've had lots of experience with reduced circumstances these past eighteen months,* he thought.

To begin his research David called the Church Support Center. He wanted to find out what normal dropout rates were. Eric Lions immediately put him at ease.

"You're going to have attrition; it's a fact of life. Up to forty percent is the estimated attrition for adult education classes. The thing to remember is that as long as you keep reaching out to new people, you'll have attrition, because not all will stay. You don't want to settle in at a hundred percent and stay there because then you'll become ingrown. In a way, adding new people causes attrition; in another way, it prevents it.

"On one hand our goal should be to keep everyone, and yet on the other hand we realize that we'll never accomplish that. 'Man's reach should exceed his grasp'—that's Alexander Pope, isn't it? Anyway, at our church we prepare our leaders not to feel like failures when people drop out, but we equip them with techniques to avoid dropouts.

"Of those who finish our six-week orientation course, almost all go on to join small groups. Then we work to keep them involved in their small group. I think the key concept is

'Use me or lose me.' Give people something to do. Make them a part of the group, a part of the action. Involvement brings commitment. At first it can be something as simple as bringing food to a meeting. As soon as they're ready, add a more important responsibility, such as a key position in the prayer chain.

"The more you reach out to people and keep in touch with them, the more they'll respond. That takes patience and persistence on the part of the leader and other group members, but it works."

While David and his group prepared their report for the church board, other groups worked on their assigned areas: growth, complaints, the comfort rut, and leader burnout.

GOOD PROBLEMS TO HAVE
◆

The way to make up for the attrition that is a natural part of life is to add new members. As some people move or drop out, new people come in to take their place. The goal should be to have more coming in than going out, so that your ministry is growing overall.

In one church a hospitality team greets newcomers at every door of the church for every service. Newcomers are introduced in each service and asked to stand so that they can be presented with a hospitality packet. While they are standing, a couple near them volunteers to be their host couple for the morning and take them for coffee in the Fellowship Hall after the service.

Newcomers are encouraged to take the orientation class that meets every Sunday evening for six weeks and covers all aspects of the church: organization, ministries, finances, doctrine, and philosophy, as well as small groups. The series is designed to explain basic New Testament church concepts and how they are employed in the local setting. At the end of the last orientation class an opportunity is given to sign up for a small group. Those who are interested fill out a membership sheet like the one on pages 93-94. They are assigned to a small group and contacted shortly thereafter. The small group is not an end in itself. Involving people in the small group is a means of involving them vitally in the church as a whole.

When the small group gets too large to meet the needs of its members or to be comfortably accommodated in a home, it multiplies. It is important to note that this process is multiplication—not division. One small group has multiplied four times. Pam Bert, the leader's wife, explained their philosophy.

"In the church we attended before coming here the small groups were so large we were told there wasn't room for us to join, so we got together with several other people for whom there wasn't room either and formed an 'un-group.' When we moved to Fellowship Bible we were determined that there would be no such thing as 'no room' in a small group.

"From the first we urged our small group members to invite others. We looked for visitors at church and invited them to our small group. We talked about evangelism at our meetings. On Sundays attenders at Fellowship Bible Church North are encouraged to wear a name tag. If you belong to a small group, your name tag will have SG on it. We looked for people without SG on their tags and invited them to join us. We planned a retreat for our small group and invited newcomers. We accepted new people from the orientation class. We did everything we could think of to reach out to others.

"And from the first we began preparing our people for multiplication. We prepared leaders to lead new groups by always having two support couples as coleaders. We gave them a lot of responsibility so people in the small group could develop loyalty to the support couples."

Pam explained how they got their support couples. "We have lots of leadership roles in our small group: group Bible study leaders, a worship leader, missions leader, mailing chairman, and others. We watch how those leaders work with people and how they accept responsibility. When we see likely leaders, we recommend them to the staff person in charge of small groups. He puts their names up for the approval of elders and staff, and they have twenty weeks of training."

Pam smiled. "It's a big deal to be a small group leader or support couple. We don't take any chances. That way we're prepared when the actual time comes to multiply. We have the support couple who will be leading the new group start leading our small group, and we talk about the multiplication two or three months ahead. This is an exciting thing, and it's important that the group perceive it as a success—as an opportunity to expand our ministry.

"We announce who the new leaders will be and give people the opportunity to choose which group they want to go with. We make clear that it's a matter of complete freedom. It's especially important for people to understand that we won't be hurt if they go with the new group—it's like sending children off to college—a sign of maturity.

"And before we multiply, we start planning a reunion for two months later. Sometimes we have a couple of reunions. Pretty soon we don't need them—the new group has outgrown the need for that support. But once every year or two we have a picnic with all our graduates. It's always so much fun to keep in touch—it's like a family reunion.

"Then when we've had a successful multiplication, we start the whole process all over again." A healthy growth group is a living, multiplying, spiritual organism.

Pam's report was so glowing that we asked her if they'd ever had a problem with their multiplication process. She gave a rueful grin. "Once. The hardest thing we ever did was to take in a 'down' small group. They were down to five couples, so we invited them to meet with us, and their leaders became our support couple."

Pam shook her head. "It sounded so reasonable, but it became a matter of 'our small group/your small group'; 'we do it this way/you do it that way'; 'we put our chairs in a row/you put your chairs in a circle.' That was the most discouraged we've ever been as small group leaders. We were afraid it wasn't going to work and that we'd have to divide rather than multiply. We just held on for four or five months and kept applying all the things we knew about reaching out in love and getting people involved. Love, prayer, and patience won the day, but we learned the hard way that that wasn't the best way to handle the situation."

We asked Pam what she saw as the key to their success. "Reaching out to others," she said. "We reach out to lots of singles, college students, and formerly marrieds. A small group can provide a good role model for younger members— especially those who aren't from Christian homes. And the younger ones are so fresh and enthusiastic that they help keep us alive. The variety of ages and backgrounds adds real spice to our small group. We find different ways to minister to them, and they minister to us in turn. All this is part of the multiplication process."

HANDLING COMPLAINTS
◆

Even the most successful small group ministry, however, will at times have to deal with complaints. As one small group member put it, "Sometimes we get on one another's nerves—like in any family."

Sometimes members have questions or suggestions for the small group. Some situations call for in-depth probing about something the small group is doing or not doing.

We've talked about leadership accountability and membership accountability. There also needs to be "churchship" accountability. Every member must have the confidence that his or her questions and probings will be received openly and handled fairly.

The key is to answer questions before they become complaints. In order to do that, Gene Getz encourages all his leaders to give their people a voice in their small group. One group designed their own survey form to encourage their people to evaluate the group, their place in it, and to express their feelings and ideas.

Leaders should report concerns regarding the ministry of the church at large to their elders and staff pastors so that they can deal with these issues. Most of the time they find that the concerns are simply related to inadequate communication. That kind of feedback helps them correct the problem. An effective small group ministry will keep the leadership of the church in tune with what people are really thinking at the grass roots level. It is a key to maintaining unity in the church at large.

SMALL GROUP SURVEY

We want to encourage ideas from small group members in order to develop a consensus on what people expect from their small groups.

Different people have different needs and different expectations, but we would like to hear what *you* think.

What is the greatest strength in your small group? _____

_____

What is the greatest weakness in your small group? _____

_____

What are the most important functions of your small group?

_____

What do you think should be required of small group members? _____

_____

What format changes may encourage more participation from the members? _____

_____

Would you like to see more variety? Explain. _____

_____

_____

Would you be willing to lead a meeting? _____
A portion of a meeting? _____
Do you have suggestions about the Bible studies or other parts of the meetings? _____

_____

_____

Do you have suggestions on how to build stronger bonds in the group such as:
    prayer partners
    active prayer chains
    monthly fellowship partners

_____

_____

_____

Is your group ministering effectively to the needs of the members? Explain. _____

_____

_____

What are some suggestions on how the group could better meet the needs of the members? _____

_____

_____

_____

Are your personal needs being met within the group? Explain. _____

_____

_____

How could your leader better minister to you? _____

_____

_____

Do you feel free to share prayer requests? _____

Do you have enough time to share prayer requests? _____

How often would you like phone calls from your leader? __

_____

Do you feel free to call your leader occasionally with prayer needs or requests, rather than waiting for his call? _____

_____

Do you want to have other activities, such as:

1) Additional meetings for men? Explain.

_____

_____

_____

_____

2) Additional meetings for women? Explain.

_____

_____

_____

_____

Other comments:

_____

_____

_____

_____

Openness and sharing ideas can prevent problems and can lead to growth in the individual and in the whole group.

HANDLING THE COMFORT TRAP

———◆———

In our illustration, when Bethany Bible Church evaluated its small group program, they found that one of their strengths was the fact that people enjoyed their small groups—they were comfortable. But at the same time, one of the problems was that people seemed to be getting too comfortable. Although the comfort rut is produced by strong bonding, commitment, and enjoyment of the small group, most of the time too much comfort leads to cliquishness.

A small group in danger of becoming a clique must reach out to others. In *A Severe Mercy* author Sheldon Vanauken quotes a letter from C. S. Lewis, warning against "a life so wholly . . . devoted to US." In speaking of the marriage relationship, Lewis warns that the "One Flesh must not (and in the long run cannot) 'live to itself' any more than a single individual." Nor can a single small group live to itself, for as Lewis warns, "To try to wrest part of the Whole [in this case, the small group] into a self-sufficing Whole [the church] on its own was 'contrary to nature'"[1] and to the law of God.

In order to avoid the comfort trap, Jim and Becki Terral warn: "Don't let your entire church life revolve around the small group. Develop relationships outside this close circle of friends. If you don't, the whole church will become a congregation of little cliques—which is the exact opposite of your goal of ministering to the whole body and building up one another.

"Plan all-church activities," the Terrals continue. "Emphasize morning worship, men's fellowship, women's fellowship, fellowship between services—every activity of the church needs support. Small groups can also get together with other small groups occasionally. After service, socialize with others in the church, don't just make a beeline for your own small group members. The pastor and small group leaders should encourage everyone to do this."

"Remember," Becki warns, "the wrong kind of relationships can kill a church as quickly as no relationships."

In addition to emphasizing the importance of relationships within the church, we always remind people to continue cultivating relationships outside the church as well. Christians need to be involved in school, community service, political, and other types of activities, both for the sake of society, where Christians are desperately needed to leaven the loaf, and for the evangelism opportunities such contacts provide. Christians need always to be growing in every area of their lives.

HANDLING LEADER BURNOUT
◆

Hard-working, dedicated leaders are the key to a successful small group program. But again, success can sow the seeds of a problem, for dedicated hard work can lead to burnout. The best way to deal with this problem is to prevent it.

In order to avoid leader burnout it's important to place as little responsibility on leaders as possible. Appoint assistant leaders, use a contract approach with leaders to make commitments for a limited time, have monthly or quarterly leadership debriefing meetings where leaders can talk with each other. It is also important for other couples in the small group to recognize their role as leader support. In Gene Getz's church, the coleaders are called "support couples," which he says is very important. No one couple should be asked to carry the leadership responsibilities alone. Perhaps the host couple could assume the role of support couple.

People need to know they are appreciated. Christians do their service for the Lord and for one another, but we're all human. Having the church sponsor an annual "Leader Appreciation Day" can let your leaders know they are appreciated and can help to prevent burnout.

Having several members of the small group join for the sole purpose of what they can get rather than what they can give promotes leader burnout. But sometimes it's a matter of the leaders demanding too much of themselves. Some overly conscientious leaders can cause their own burnout. One leader couple told us of their experience. "We asked the group what they wanted in terms of Bible study, fellowship, and outreach projects; then we set about to provide it all. We were doing almost all of the work. After a year of that pace we were approaching burnout.

"We told the group just how we felt. They had had no idea. They volunteered to help take over the fellowship time, responsibility for hosting, outreach projects, things like that. Now attendance is better because the people are more involved. The key was being open with them."

Gene Getz's church uses a two-stage program to prevent leader burnout. First, they have an ongoing program of training new leaders and support leaders so people are always available to help share the load when they're needed. Second, they have a well-developed program of care pastors and care group meetings to support their leaders.

Leadership Development Program

In order to avoid leadership burnout, it's important to select and prepare new leaders constantly. Fellowship Bible Church's small group leadership development program is a rather extensive educational training process centered on the three vital experiences necessary for spiritual growth and maturity: doctrine, human relations, and evangelism. The main purpose of the training class is to disciple and prepare potential leaders. This is accomplished both by furthering potential leaders in their own spiritual maturity and by preparing them for small group ministry.

The program begins with the leadership selection process. In June the church office sends a mailing to all small group leaders that includes a cover letter outlining the process for recommendation and selection of leader candidates, a small group leader job description, guidelines for small group leaders, and a recommendation form.

The next step is to present the couples who have been recommended to the staff and elders for approval, and the staff and elders may add or remove names. All couples on the approved list are interviewed to determine their relationship to Jesus Christ and their relative maturity before invitations are issued to the training series. Note: This process must be kept confidential among small group leaders and the church staff.

All couples on the approved list receive letters inviting them to attend the training class, which begins in September. At the same time elders, staff, and small group leaders receive letters announcing the new small group leadership class and a list of the approved couples who have agreed to attend the training.

Note: Attending the leadership training classes does not guarantee a position of leadership in a small group. This does not commit those in training to accept a position nor does it commit the church to offer a position.

It is essential to be committed to a ministry of encouragement to your leaders. Of primary importance is regular communication with them. Besides the small group support and giving leaders general encouragement, support activities might be divided into two categories: practical and emotional. In the practical area, provide your leaders with materials (see Appendix B) to try to help them keep the prep time for each meeting as low as possible, and hold leadership seminars perhaps twice a year. On the emotional side, make your leaders feel needed. Most leaders love their job. But they must also have the freedom to step aside. Part of leadership support is teaching them when to let go.

The Next Generation

Remember Jared Flavell and his comment that he didn't have one real friend at church? We looked at Fellowship Bible Church North to see how they use the small group concept to meet the universal need teens have for friends. The overall focus of their teen ministry is relational. "Spending time with kids is what makes it all happen," teen pastors Dave Shaw and Jack Warren stated.

Dave continued, "In our senior high ministry we meet with the whole group on Sunday mornings and Wednesday nights. We also have several big events a year such as a fun time at Six Flags Over Texas, or a retreat to a mountain lodge, or a beach party designed so they can bring friends for evangelism. At these all-group events our staff members identify teens to invite to participate in small groups. We look for kids who show commitment.

"Right now we have five senior high growth groups. They meet twice a month in teen homes with a staff leader for Bible study, sharing, and evangelism—and always refreshments, of course. Rotating homes is important because this is a good way for staff members to get to know the teens' parents and for the parents to meet their son's or daughter's friends.

"We find significant bonding in these small groups, both among the teens themselves and between the teens and their leaders. When teens in a growth group have problems or questions, they go to their small group leaders."

Because it's difficult for junior highers to go out at night, their groups are less formal. "We call them contact groups," Jack Warren explains. "We divide all the kids into groups of eight or ten, each with an adult volunteer leader. The leader contacts everyone in the group once a month. Sometimes it's just a phone call to say, 'How's it going?' Sometimes they take them out for ice cream or a Coke®—either as a whole group or one-on-one."

And again significant bonding takes place in these small groups. Teens identify with their group and go to their staff person with their needs.

"Because ninth grade is a bridge age between junior and senior high, we have a special program for them—faith groups. Faith groups meet every Sunday night in someone's home, usually in groups of fifteen to twenty teens. We have fifteen minutes of recreation, forty-five minutes of Bible study and discussion, then break into small groups of two or three for sharing and prayer. And then refreshments—can't ever forget that.

"Our senior high leaders emerge from these faith groups, and adult leaders emerge from our senior high growth groups. This way our total church program lays the groundwork for leadership development and for keeping the ongoing ministry of the church strong."

With similar programs teens like Jared Flavell can bond in close relationships with peers who have the same values and can form friendships that may last for life.

With active planning for the future such as we've outlined in this chapter, with group multiplication, ongoing leadership training, and preparation of teens to step right into the small group ministry, the long-term health of your groups can be assured. We hope this will be of special encouragement to anyone who, like Susan Flavell's friend Betty Jo, has tried programs that were less than successful, or to anyone who fears taking the first-time plunge because he worries that the small group phenomenon might turn out to be a "modern fad"—a misapprehension we love to answer by pointing out that since such a concern didn't stop Jesus from forming a small group, it shouldn't stop us.

CHAPTER ELEVEN

Looking Ahead

*D*avid looked around the circle of fire-lit faces. He suddenly saw clearly how dear these people had become to him. For a whole year now they had shared together, prayed together, struggled together, grown together. Although he didn't have a brother in his family, he was sure this was the true fellowship that Proverbs 18:24 spoke of as being "closer than a brother." In their small group they had truly become members of one another.

To celebrate their year of being together, the Flavell small group had decided to go on a weekend retreat. Since it was off-season, the rates at Blue Lake Lodge were reasonable, and after a two and a half hour drive they were all sitting in front of a roaring fire in a huge, stone fireplace in the rustic, open-beamed lounge of the mountain retreat. They had all eaten their fill of spicy chili and crusty loaves of French bread, and the atmosphere couldn't have been better for relaxed, open sharing.

David opened his Bible and read Romans 15:5: "Now may the God who gives perseverance and encouragement grant you to be of the same mind with one another according to Christ Jesus." He laid the Bible on the arm of his over-stuffed chair. "I am so thankful that God has brought us together this year and that He has given us the unity and oneness Paul prays for in this verse. All around us we see a fragmented, isolated world, but in Christ we are brought together in unity. I thank God, and I thank each of you. And I want us to spend time this evening sharing what this unity, this togetherness, has meant in our lives these past months."

Outside, the wind blew through the tall pine trees behind the lodge, and waves lapped the sandy beach below, but inside, the fire crackled warmly, and all in its circle drew together. Several smiled, recalling events of the past year, but no one spoke for some time as if none wanted to break the atmosphere. At last Mitzi gave a nervous giggle. "Well, I guess I'll go first." But having said that, she was quiet for a moment, running her long, red fingernails through her spiked hair as if gathering her courage. "I guess most of you know I wasn't exactly raising my daughter, Lara, in a model Christian home, even though I did bring her to Sunday school sometimes. Then Debbie Flavell became her friend, and pretty soon I got mixed up in this small group thing." She paused while everyone laughed. "And all of a sudden I saw a whole new kind of life. And you know what I appreciated most? No one ever said to me, 'Honey, you gotta clean up your act.' You just loved me and showed me a better way to live."

This time she stopped to sniff. "I'm not exactly a saint yet—I doubt I ever will be—but I sure do know a lot of saints now, and—well, I guess what I'm trying to say is that I really want to grow. I still can't believe it! I bet a whole bunch of you were praying for me behind my back—huh?"

The response around the room was loving and gently humorous. Mitzi grinned. "Yeah, I thought so. Well, keep it up."

Janice Croft sat in the only rocker in the room with baby Sean snuggled in her arms. She was still nursing him, so he had come on the retreat, too. "You know," she said, "a year ago I was really lonesome. It was like Leon and Erin and I were on a desert island. And I wanted to call my family back in Iowa so bad, but I didn't dare because I knew I'd just cry.

"And then Susan invited us to the small group—and suddenly we had a whole family. Now look—Sean has Uncle Jerry and Aunt Anna, and Uncle Al and Aunt Karen, and Uncle Bo and Aunt Tessa—you're all our extended family—that's more aunts and uncles than we have back in Iowa."

Sean stirred and whimpered. Al, sitting next to them, laid his big hand on the soft, warm head. "I hope he's not wanting Uncle Al to change his diapers." Everyone chuckled. Then Al began to talk. "Well, I guess you know, I—we, really," he looked at Karen sitting on his left, "were in pretty bad shape a year ago. I can't tell you that everything's perfect now and always will be, but I can report that with your support I haven't missed an AA meeting in seven months now—and that's the longest I've been dry since I was in high school. And Karen's been going to Al-Anon with Tessa, and—well, like I said, everything isn't perfect, but we're working on it. I know if it hadn't been for all you guys, we wouldn't be sitting here—or anywhere else—together tonight." Karen leaned across the arm of her chair and squeezed her husband's hand.

The sharing went on around the circle, crisscrossing back and forth until everyone who wanted to had had a chance to talk. Then it was back to David and Susan. "Well, I hope you know you've kept us going this year, too. I think the hardest thing I ever did was telling Susan to tell you about our business problems—so much of a man's ego is tied up in his business, you know. But we've sure appreciated your prayers and concern—the jobs Karen gave Susan and Jared at Christmas, the groceries—but most of all just showing that you didn't think we were worthless just because our bank account was.

"And I've been saving a bit of good news—you can't imagine how hard it was not to tell Susan on the drive up here, but I wanted to share it with you all together—a couple of weeks ago I lost a bid to build a convenience store. It was a real squeaker—but you know, close only counts in horseshoes. Then, just before I left the office today, they called and said they'd discovered that the company who won the bid wasn't planning to use the quality of materials they wanted in the job—so we're getting it after all!"

"Oh, David!" Susan almost knocked her chair over as she flung herself into his arms. "Oh, praise the Lord!" She looked around the group. "You guys were praying for us behind our backs, too—huh?"

Susan knew, as David had explained to her when he figured the bid, that this job wouldn't pay off any of their debt from the Megacorp disaster, but it would ensure that they wouldn't have to try to borrow more just to keep going. Clearly God was working.

Then, with the moon just peeking over the mountains on the far side of the lake and shining through the floor-to-ceiling windows, the group began their prayer time. There were many, many praises and also many requests. As each item was mentioned, someone in the group raised a hand to volunteer to pray for that person. Susan spoke last. "As most of you know, my Uncle Clarence—my only living relative—had a heart attack right after Christmas, and he's been living with us while he recovers. He'd been doing lots better, and I think he still is—the doctor seems pleased—but just before we left this afternoon, I went in to his room to tell him good-bye. He was sitting all cozy in his big easy chair with his feet propped up on a stool under a quilt reading his Bible." The vivid memory choked her, and she stopped. "He looked so—so beautiful and fragile. And he said, 'Susan, pray the Lord will take me—I want to go home.'"

It was several moments before Susan could control her voice enough to continue. "I hugged him and told him I didn't want him to go—but I'm afraid—"

SETTING YOUR GOALS
♦

Let's leave the Flavell small group praying for one another while we look at where God is leading us. What does He want us to do about the ideas we've set forth in this book? A small group retreat looks both backward and forward: backward to the New Testament with the disciples waiting in the Upper Room, and forward to the fulfillment of that waiting when He comes again and we will share together in heaven. But our discussion must be regarding what we are to do here and now.

Through the small group, we act out three of Christ's most important statements:

A new commandment I give to you, that you love one another. (John 13:34*a*)
As I have loved you, . . . you also love one another. (John 13:34*b*)
All men will know that you are My disciples, if you have love for one another. (John 13:35)

Christ's basic concern in each of those statements was our love for one another. But each statement also contains a special emphasis. First, to love one another was a new commandment. Second, Christ's love for the disciples was to be their model for loving one another. And third, that love was to be the means whereby the apostles could communicate to all men the One whom they were emulating in their relationships.[1]

And that is the purpose of all this—of caring for one another, of small groups, of this book—so that the world will know that Jesus Christ is Lord. That's why the church exists in the first place. The ultimate goal of the small group is to expose people who don't know Jesus Christ to His love. We have small groups so the world can see Christ fleshed out. It's our way of taking Christ to the world. It's a lot of work, but when you see people coming to the Lord, it's worth it. There's no greater task.

Allen Doran focused on the inward, nurturing aspect of the small group when he described the small group as a lovely, peaceful, green oasis with couples quietly and safely sharing in the midst of an ugly, damaged, polluted city. One of his favorite books as a child was *The Secret Garden*. That's what a small group can be—a holding environment, a safe enclosure from the sin around us. In a safe place we can unite as Christ intended. We need to share our lives with one another, support each other, and grow in the Lord as true spiritual beings. From that base we can go forth to carry out the Great Commission.

The holes in our souls can be filled through a small group ministry. That is what we need to be more effective for Christ. It's what the church needs to be effective in ministering to its people. It's what the community needs so they can come to the Lord through seeing love in action.

We need a revolution. Let's quit hiding behind pews and smiles, get into small groups, and work on who we are from the inside out instead of focusing on legalistic or external behavior. We are all people in process, so we need to pick

each other up and keep on going. When we become the most functional Christians we can be, others will see and join us.

That's our quiet revolution—the revolution of love that Jesus Christ started.

The Flavells sat in their living room surrounded by friends from their small group after Uncle Clarence's funeral. "It was beautiful," Susan said. "Just the home-going he would have wanted. He always said he didn't want a eulogy or anything about him at his funeral—just lots of Scripture and hymns."

"'Amazing Grace' was beautiful," Karen said. "I want it played on the bagpipes at my funeral."

Al made a face and covered his ears. "Oooh, you'd better outlive me, then, because it'd sure look strange if I didn't go to your funeral!"

Tessa passed around cups of coffee as Bo answered the door when the bell rang. A moment later David called Susan into his office. "This is Ted Morrison, Clarence's lawyer. I told him it'd be all right to drop by this afternoon."

Susan hardly listened to the details of insurance and property the two men were discussing, but she sat up straight when Mr. Morrison brought out a will. "How silly of me—I never thought—of course he would have a will. I suppose just about everyone does, but he didn't have enough property to worry about, did he?"

"Not what I suppose you'd call a big estate, but when his house is sold and his bills paid, it looks like you should have about twenty-five thousand dollars."

Susan sat stunned. The Lord had provided. Every step of the way, to the last penny. There had always been food on the table, the kids had had new shoes, they even had Christmas presents—and now He had provided the exact amount they needed to get out of debt. With her face shining, she stood up. "Excuse me, I want to share this with my family."

As she went out, the lawyer frowned. "I thought Clarence was her last living relative—oh, I suppose she means your children."

David smiled. "No, she means our extended family out there."

But before Susan could say anything, the doorbell rang again. Jared walked through the living room to answer it and reappeared a minute later with two T-shirt- and sneaker-clad boys who looked much like himself. "Mom, meet Bob and Matt—my two best friends from church."

Outwardly Susan greeted them, but inside she was saying, *Thank you, Lord. My cup runneth over.*

APPENDIX A

Style of Influence Questionnaire

*T*he Style of Influence (SOI) Questionnaire is based on a four-factor model of leadership and influence. It was researched and developed by Doug Wilson and Gene Getz. The information provided here defines the four scales used in the survey and has been modified slightly.

COGNITIVE STYLE

◆

A Concrete Orientation

Concrete thinkers are good organizers of others' ideas. They are concerned about whether an idea is practical and relevant to the masses. They will often ask tough questions that frustrate the "blue sky" thinker but which do, indeed, need to be addressed.

On the other hand, concrete thinkers evaluate their world tightly. They assume a conservative approach to new ideas and may have difficulty discriminating between the principle behind an idea and the idea itself. More specifically, concrete thinkers do not naturally and spontaneously discriminate between what is form and what is function. Function relates to the principle behind an idea. Form relates to how the idea takes shape in a specific setting.

An Abstract Orientation

Abstract thinkers are designers and philosophical thinkers. They actually enjoy ambiguity and can live comfortably in this kind of arena.

Abstract thinkers, on the other hand, may face difficulty nailing down ideas into concrete statements that are useful to others. That is one reason abstract thinkers need assistance from concrete thinkers.

A Concrete-Abstract Orientation

Individuals who score mid-range want to make abstract ideas practical. They want to know, "How does the principle work?" However, at times they may jump to hasty conclusions before evaluating all the ramifications of an idea. Usually "middle of the roaders" work best with abstract thinkers who create new ideas. They then can interact with those ideas and seek creative ways to implement them. They can also help concrete thinkers to understand better what abstract thinkers desire to achieve in the organization.

RELATIONAL STYLE

A Tough-Minded Orientation

Tough-minded individuals enjoy difficult tasks. They like to see results. They are capable of real friendships and caring but may lack a deep empathy for another person's orientation.

Tough-minded persons usually do not work hard at understanding others' feelings. Though they may want to be understanding, they do not find this a natural tendency. Tough-minded people believe that others are present to do a job or perform a function. If a coworker has personal problems, tough-minded persons can be very friendly but may not understand the problem at an emotional level.

A Supportive Orientation

Highly supportive individuals naturally make strong efforts to provide encouragement and believe the best about a person. They may not always be aware of what another person is feeling, but they usually work at demonstrating warmth and an attitude that says "I care." They can easily become subjectively involved in trying to help someone in the organization who is struggling.

Individuals who score in the middle on this scale are supportive but at times are less sensitive to the needs of others. They desire to communicate support, yet tend to be more tough-minded. Because of their dual tendencies, they can help tough-minded people be more understanding and sensitive, and they can help highly supportive people to be more objective and, when necessary, more confrontational.

GOAL ACHIEVEMENT STYLE

◆

High Task Orientation

Individuals who score high on this scale naturally desire to take charge and make things happen. They feel personally responsible for the accomplishment of an objective. They are ambitious and "have a nose" for opportunity. They often want to lead and can function independently. Recognition and challenge are high motivators. These people literally "attack" a task head-on.

Low Task Orientation

Individuals who score low on this scale also enjoy a challenge but are more compliant and desirous of following another person's lead. They are more mild-mannered and easy-going.

They may indeed enjoy a flurry of activity but normally desire clear communication of other people's expectations. They do not want to be primarily responsible for ultimate outcomes.

High Task-Low Task Orientation

People who have a moderate score on this scale are ambitious but less direct in how they go about accomplishing tasks. They are relaxed but tend to take a passive approach to leadership. They may find it difficult to make hard decisions, exercise extreme discipline, or confront others to move a task forward.

Moderate scorers usually complement a person who scores high on this scale as long as they do not feel put down or "less than" for not being as ambitious. They are usually very task-oriented but also see themselves in supportive roles to others who are taking the final responsibility for a team.

DETAIL STYLE

High Preference Orientation

Those who give high attention to detail want everything well-organized. In fact, they tend to border on perfectionism. They enjoy organizing information accurately, they plan well, and they keep everything tidy in the process. However, they must be on guard against losing sight of the big picture, seeing only the "trees" and not the "forest."

Highly detailed individuals may be somewhat insensitive to their own personal needs. Sometimes they work out feelings of insecurity by always being organized and controlled.

Low Preference Orientation

Those who record a low preference for detail may tend to be restless and appear to be disorganized. They must work hard at not neglecting important dimensions of a project that requires attention to detail.

On the other hand, people who score low on detail usually have the ability to delegate. If they use this skill effectively, their performance will not necessarily be lacking.

High Preference-Low Preference Orientation

Those with moderate attention to detail can easily plan a project and manage the necessary components for the administration of the project. They may not immensely enjoy organization and follow-through, but they have a sense of internal discipline that pushes them through the stages of design and implementation that require attention to detail.

Although there is no perfect "pattern of influence," certain patterns are more effective for certain situations. In taking the SOI, individuals will hopefully grow in the following four areas:

- personal awareness of giftedness (talents)
- the need for versatility or further growth
- an awareness of potential conflict areas
- an understanding of other styles of influence

To obtain a copy of the Style of Influence Questionnaire, please write:

Center for Church Renewal
200 Chisholm Place, Suite 228
Plano, TX 75075
(213) 423-4262

APPENDIX B

Body Builder Lessons

*T*hese Body Builder lessons, written by Marty Younkin for use at Fellowship Bible Church North, are sample studies for your small group.

Lesson 1   Colossians 1:1-14

PERSONALIZATION

What is one positive trait or attitude your father has passed on to you? How did he transmit this to you?

EDIFICATION

Paul, an apostle of Jesus Christ by the will of God, and Timothy our brother, to the saints and faithful brethren in Christ who are at Colossae: Grace to you and peace from God our Father. We give thanks to God, the Father of our Lord Jesus Christ, praying always for you, since we heard of your faith in Christ Jesus and the love which you have for all the saints; because of the hope laid up for you in heaven, of which you previously heard in the word of truth, the gospel, which has come to you, just as in all the world also it is constantly bearing fruit and increasing, even as it has been doing in you also since the day you heard of it and understood the grace of God in truth; just as you learned it from Epaphras, our beloved fellow bondservant, who is a faithful servant of Christ on our behalf, and he also informed us of your love in the Spirit.

For this reason also, since the day we heard of it, we have not ceased to pray for you and to ask that you may be filled with the knowledge of His will in all spiritual wisdom and understanding, so that you may walk in a manner worthy of the Lord, to please Him in all respects, bearing fruit in every good work and increasing in the knowledge of God; strengthened with all power, according to His glorious might, for the attaining of all steadfastness and patience; joyously giving thanks to the Father, who has qualified us to share in the inheritance of the saints in light. For He delivered us from the domain of darkness, and transferred us to the kingdom of His beloved Son, in whom we have redemption, the forgiveness of sins. (Col. 1:1-14)

1. How does Paul describe the people he's writing to?
2. How would you characterize Paul's concern for these people whom he has never met?
3. Why do you think he has such great concern for them?
4. What does this tell you about Paul?
5. What does this tell you about how Christians should feel about others?
6. According to verses 10-12, what are the marks of the Christian?
7. How do these traits relate to one another?
8. Why would Paul be so concerned that the Colossians have these qualities in their lives?

APPLICATION
———◆———

1. How does your style of prayer compare with the one described here—in thankfulness, in intensity, in consistency, in praying for other believers?
2. What has God taught you about prayer recently?
3. What does the spiritual crop in your life look like?
4. How are you bearing fruit?
5. What does the Farmer need to do to make you more fruitful?
6. In verses 10-12, Paul discusses Christian maturity. How well are you doing in the areas he mentions?
7. How can you show your Christian concern for people you have never met?
8. Will you start doing this today? Why or why not?

LESSONS FOR LIVING
———◆———

Memorize Colossians 1:9-10.

Pray each day this week for Colossians 1:9-10 to be realized in your own life.

Lesson 2   Colossians 1:15-23

PERSONALIZATION

——♦——

When you were a child, around whom did your family revolve? Why? What does that say about your family?

EDIFICATION

——♦——

And He is the image of the invisible God, the first-born of all creation. For by Him all things were created, both in the heavens and on earth, visible and invisible, whether thrones or dominions or rulers or authorities—all things have been created by Him and for Him. And He is before all things, and in Him all things hold together. He is also head of the body, the church; and He is the beginning, the first-born from the dead; so that He Himself might come to have first place in everything. For it was the Father's good pleasure for all the fulness to dwell in Him, and through Him to reconcile all things to Himself, having made peace through the blood of His cross; through Him, I say, whether things on earth or things in heaven.

And although you were formerly alienated and hostile in mind, engaged in evil deeds, yet He has now reconciled you in His fleshly body through death, in order to present you before Him holy and blameless and beyond reproach—if indeed you continue in the faith firmly established and steadfast, and not moved away from the hope of the gospel that you have heard, which was proclaimed in all creation under heaven, and of which I, Paul, was made a minister. (Col. 1:15-23)

1. How many characteristics of Christ are noted in verses 15-20?
2. How would you describe each of them?

3. How would you summarize these six jam-packed verses in ten words?
4. What does it mean to be alienated from God?
5. What is the gospel? How has it reconciled us to God?

APPLICATION

1. What do the attributes of Christ mentioned in verses 15-20 mean to you?
2. How do they affect your relationship with Jesus?
3. What does reconciliation mean to you? How are you more reconciled (with God, family, coworkers, believers) now than you've been in the past?
4. How are you less reconciled?
5. How can your Christian friends pray for you in this area?
6. Have you ever felt alienated from God or family or friends or coworkers or other believers? If so, when? What were the circumstances? How were you reconciled?
7. In what area of your life do you have the most difficulty giving Christ supremacy? Why? What will you do today to begin eliminating this difficulty?

LESSONS FOR LIVING

Memorize Colossians 1:17.

Write down the ways God has kept your life together or kept your life from falling apart. Spend time each day thanking Him.

Lesson 3   Colossians 1:24–2:5

PERSONALIZATION
◆

What was one of the toughest times in your life, and how did it affect you? What was one of the most terrific times in your life, and how did it affect you?

EDIFICATION
◆

Now I rejoice in my sufferings for your sake, and in my flesh I do my share on behalf of His body (which is the church) in filling up that which is lacking in Christ's afflictions. Of this church I was made a minister according to the stewardship from God bestowed on me for your benefit, that I might fully carry out the preaching of the word of God, that is, the mystery which has been hidden from the past ages and generations; but has now been manifested to His saints, to whom God willed to make known what is the riches of the glory of this mystery among the Gentiles, which is Christ in you, the hope of glory.

And we proclaim Him, admonishing every man and teaching every man with all wisdom, that we may present every man complete in Christ. And for this purpose also I labor, striving according to His power, which mightily works within me.

For I want you to know how great a struggle I have on your behalf, and for those who are at Laodicea, and for all those who have not personally seen my face, that their hearts may be encouraged, having been knit together in love, and attaining to all the wealth that comes from the full assurance of understanding, resulting in a true knowledge of God's mystery, that is, Christ Himself, in whom are hidden all the treasures of wisdom and knowledge. I say this in order that no one may delude you with persuasive argument. For even though I am absent in body, nevertheless I am with you in spirit, rejoicing to see your good discipline and the stability of your faith in Christ. (Col. 1:24–2:5)

1. In what sense could Paul suffer for Christians he did not know?
2. Why would he want to suffer for them? What does that tell you about Paul?
3. What does "Christ in you" mean?
4. Why does Paul consider this a mystery? How does it give hope?
5. What are the themes of verses 1:15–2:5?
6. What are the probable arguments these themes would refute (v. 4)?
7. What do you learn about the Colossian church from this?

APPLICATION
◆

1. Paul uses words such as *suffer, struggle,* and *labor.* Did you imagine the Christian life would be that tough when you became a believer?
2. Is the Christian life what you expected it would be?
3. How is the Christian life a mystery to you? Does the fact that it is a mystery bother you? Why or why not?
4. In what way has Colossians spoken to problems that you may be encountering in your life at this time?
5. Have you taken any actions? Have your actions helped or hindered your progress in your Christian walk?

LESSONS FOR LIVING
——◆——

Memorize Colossians 1:28.

Sit down with a friend and establish some attainable goals so that you can see progress in your Christian life. Get together weekly with your friend to evaluate and be accountable.

Notes

Chapter 3: Producing a Mature Church

1. John Stott, "Setting the Spirit Free," *Christianity Today,* June 12, 1981, p. 18.
2. Thomas Merton, *Praying the Psalms* (Collegeville, Minn.: Liturgical, 1956), pp. 7-9.
3. Gene Getz, One Another series (Wheaton, Ill.: Victor): *Building Up One Another* (1976), *Encouraging One Another* (1981), *Loving One Another* (1979), *Praying for One Another* (1982), and *Serving One Another* (1984).

Chapter 4: Laying the Groundwork 1: Leadership

1. If your church would like to have a similar worker with you for a weekend, call the Center for Church Renewal in Plano, Texas, at (214) 423-4262.
2. See Ray Stedman's *Body Life*, rev. ed. (Ventura, Calif.: Regal, 1979); Gene Getz's *Sharpening the Focus of the Church* (Wheaton, Ill.: Victor, 1984); or "Biblical Renewal" videotape series, based on *Sharpening the Focus of the Church*, available from Center for Church Renewal, 200 Chisholm Place, Suite 228, Plano, Texas 75075, (214) 423-4262.
3. On this and other models Gene Getz prefers to call the small groups "minichurches" because he sees them as small churches—groups that give the participants the same experiences the church was scripturally intended to give: Bible doctrine, fellowship, and evangelism.

Chapter 5: Laying the Groundwork 2: Logistics

1. For more information call Serendipity toll-free, (800) 525-9563; or Navigators, (719) 598-1212.

Chapter 7: Experiencing the Small Group

1. For more information, write: Serendipity House, Box 1012, Littleton, CO 80160, or call toll-free, 800-525-9563, for a catalog.
2. Roberta Hestenes, *Using the Bible in Groups* (Philadelphia: Westminster, 1983), p. 107.

Chapter 10: Coping with Success

1. Sheldon Vanauken, *A Severe Mercy* (San Franciso: Harper & Row, 1977), p. 209.

Chapter 11: Looking Ahead

1. Gene A. Getz, *Loving One Another* (Wheaton, Ill.: Victor, 1979), p. 12.

Recommended Reading

Coleman, Lyman. *Training Manual for Groups*. Henderson, Nev.: Serendipity, 1991.

Corey, Marianne Schneider, and Gerald Corey. *Groups, Process and Practice*. Pacific Grove, Calif.: Brooks/Cole, 1986.

Getz, Gene. One Another Series (Wheaton, Ill.: Victor): *Building Up One Another* (1976), *Encouraging One Another* (1981), *Loving One Another* (1979), *Praying for One Another* (1982), *Serving One Another* (1984).

_____. The Measure of Series (Ventura, Calif.: Regal): *The Measure of a Church* (1975), *The Measure of a Family* (1976), *The Measure of a Man* (1974), *The Measure of a Marriage* (1980), *The Measure of a Woman* (1977).

_____. *Sharpening the Focus of the Church*. Wheaton, Ill.: Victor, 1984.

Hemfelt, Robert, and Frank Minirth. *We Are Driven*. Nashville: Thomas Nelson, 1991.

Meier, Paul, and Frank Minirth. *Free to Forgive*. Nashville: Thomas Nelson, 1991.

Minirth, Frank, Don Hawkins, Paul Meier, and Richard Flournoy. *How to Beat Burnout*. Chicago: Moody, 1986.

Minirth, Frank, Don Hawkins, Paul Meier, and Chris Thurman. *Before Burnout*. Chicago: Moody, 1990.

Minirth, Frank, Richard Meier, Paul Meier, and Don Hawkins. *The Healthy Christian Life*. Grand Rapids: Baker, 1988.

Moody Press, a ministry of the Moody Bible Institute,
is designed for education, evangelization, and edification.
If we may assist you in knowing more about Christ
and the Christian life, please write us without obligation:
Moody Press, c/o MLM, Chicago, Illinois 60610.